Entrepreneurship in Indonesia

Whilst other countries in Asia particularly China and India have been studied in terms of entrepreneurial endeavours, there is a lack of research on Indonesia despite it being amongst the fastest growing economies in the world. Indonesia is also one of the largest recipients of venture capital in Asia. This book looks at the growth of entrepreneurship in Indonesia from artisan and cultural endeavours to an increased awareness of digital and technology-based forms of entrepreneurship.

The book examines the distinct cultural heritage of people in Indonesia towards entrepreneurial pursuits and analyses the role family and minority businesses play in the development of entrepreneurial capabilities. It stresses the need to focus on more categories of entrepreneurship in Indonesia such as artisan, tourism and sustainability in order to facilitate the growth of digital-based startups.

This book will be amongst the first to explore how Indonesia is leaping ahead of competitors in its quest to be a dominant world power through its entrepreneurial pursuits.

Vanessa Ratten is an Associate Professor at La Trobe University, Australia.

Routledge Studies in Entrepreneurship

This series extends the meaning and scope of entrepreneurship by capturing new research and enquiry on economic, social, cultural and personal value creation. Entrepreneurship as value creation represents the endeavours of innovative people and organisations in creative environments that open up opportunities for developing new products, new services, new firms and new forms of policy making in different environments seeking sustainable economic growth and social development. In setting this objective the series includes books which cover a diverse range of conceptual, empirical and scholarly topics that both inform the field and push the boundaries of entrepreneurship.

Entrepreneurship in Spain
A History
Edited by Juan Manuel Matés-Barco and Leonardo Caruana de las Cagigas

Women and Global Entrepreneurship
Contextualising Everyday Experiences
Edited by Maura McAdam and James A. Cunningham

Digital Entrepreneurship and the Sharing Economy
Edited by Evgueni Vinogradov, Birgit Leick and Djamchid Assadi

Entrepreneurship in India
Alexander Newman, Andrea North-Samardzic, Madhura Bedarkar and Yogesh Brahmankar

Entrepreneurship in Indonesia
From Artisan and Tourism to Technology-based Business Growth
Edited by Vanessa Ratten

For more information about this series please visit: www.routledge.com/Routledge-Studies-in-Entrepreneurship/book-series/RSE

Entrepreneurship in Indonesia

From Artisan and Tourism to Technology-based Business Growth

Edited by Vanessa Ratten

LONDON AND NEW YORK

First published 2022
by Routledge
2 Park Square, Milton Park, Abingdon, Oxon OX14 4RN

and by Routledge
605 Third Avenue, New York, NY 10158

Routledge is an imprint of the Taylor & Francis Group, an informa business

© 2022 selection and editorial matter, Vanessa Ratten; individual chapters, the contributors

The right of Vanessa Ratten to be identified as the author of the editorial material, and of the authors for their individual chapters, has been asserted in accordance with sections 77 and 78 of the Copyright, Designs and Patents Act 1988.

All rights reserved. No part of this book may be reprinted or reproduced or utilised in any form or by any electronic, mechanical, or other means, now known or hereafter invented, including photocopying and recording, or in any information storage or retrieval system, without permission in writing from the publishers.

Trademark notice: Product or corporate names may be trademarks or registered trademarks, and are used only for identification and explanation without intent to infringe.

British Library Cataloguing-in-Publication Data
A catalogue record for this book is available from the British Library

Library of Congress Cataloging-in-Publication Data
Names: Ratten, Vanessa, editor.
Title: Entrepreneurship in Indonesia : from artisan and tourism to
   technology-based business growth / edited by Vanessa Ratten.
Description: Abingdon, Oxon ; New York, NY : Routledge,
   2022. | Series: Routledge studies in entrepreneurship | Includes
   bibliographical references and index.
Identifiers: LCCN 2021022155 (print) | LCCN 2021022156
   (ebook)
Subjects: LCSH: Entrepreneurship—Indonesia. | Economic
   development—Indonesia.
Classification: LCC HC447 .E575 2022 (print) | LCC HC447
   (ebook) | DDC 338/.0409598—dc23
LC record available at https://lccn.loc.gov/2021022155
LC ebook record available at https://lccn.loc.gov/2021022156

ISBN: 9781032035246 (hbk)
ISBN: 9781032035253 (pbk)
ISBN: 9781003187769 (ebk)

DOI: 10.4324/9781003187769

Typeset in Galliard
by Apex CoVantage, LLC

Contents

List of Tables vii
List of Figures viii
Acknowledgements ix
List of Contributors x

1 Indonesian entrepreneurship: origins, conceptualisation
  and practice 1
  VANESSA RATTEN

2 Artisan entrepreneurship in Indonesia 14
  VANESSA RATTEN

3 Food artisan entrepreneurship in Indonesia 32
  VANESSA RATTEN

4 Knowledge management and artisan entrepreneurship
  in Indonesia 45
  VANESSA RATTEN

5 Indonesian migrant entrepreneurs: a comparison of two
  cohorts in Malaysia 57
  HAMIZAH ABD HAMID

6 Technology entrepreneurship in Indonesia 78
  VANESSA RATTEN

7 Cross-sectional study (period 2013–2016) of the factors that
  identify entrepreneurship in Indonesia 92
  MERCEDES BARRACHINA FERNÁNDEZ, MARIA DEL CARMEN
  GARCIA CENTENO AND CARMEN CALDERÓN PATIER

8	**Rural entrepreneurship and social innovation in Indonesia** VANESSA RATTEN	103
9	**Indonesian entrepreneurship: Future directions** VANESSA RATTEN	114
	Index	132

Tables

1.1	Major environmental effects on Indonesian entrepreneurship	6
2.1	Framework for Indonesian artisan entrepreneurship research	21
2.2	Types of Indonesian handicrafts	27
5.1	Sources of primary data for the study	63
5.2	Summary of supplementary respondents	64
5.3	Summary of the findings	71
7.1	Description of variables	96
7.2	Results obtained from the logistic regression	98
9.1	Suggestions for future research on Indonesian entrepreneurship in contextual terms	123
9.2	Future research areas for Indonesian entrepreneurship	126

Figures

5.1 Migration from Indonesia to Malaysia 61
5.2 The embeddedness of the migration and entrepreneurial activities 74

Acknowledgements

I thank Yongling Lam for her help and advice in editing this book about Indonesian entrepreneurship that focuses on how it has transformed to be focused both on artisan and technology ventures. Indonesia has always fascinated me. When I started my first year of high school, I chose to study Bahasa Indonesian instead of the other European languages on offer. The reason for this was due to my mum's interest in Asia especially given Indonesia's close geographical position to Australia. This was a good decision as I learnt to love the language and the culture. Fortunately, when my family moved from Melbourne to Brisbane my mum researched schools that taught both Indonesian and Japanese so I was able to continue my studies. I was very lucky that my mum did this as there were only two schools at the time that taught both languages and only one near the city centre. My mum had the foresight to think about the importance of Indonesia in the global economy and particularly for Australia which is located close to Indonesia. I also continued my studies on Bahasa Indonesian at The University of Queensland in conjunction with studying Mandarin. I ended up receiving a Bachelor of Arts (majoring in Economics and Mandarin) in addition to my other degrees. Thus, I dedicate this book to my mum Kaye Ratten. I also thank my other family members David, Stuart, Hamish, Tomomi and Sakura Ratten.

Contributors

Maria del Carmen Garcia Centeno is a Professor at San Pablo CEU University, Spain.

Mercedes Barrachina Fernández is a Professor at San Pablo CEU University, Spain.

Hamizah Abd Hamid is a Lecturer at the Universiti Kebangsaan Malaysia, Malaysia.

Carmen Calderón Patier is a Professor at San Pablo CEU University, Spain.

Vanessa Ratten is an Associate Professor at La Trobe University, Australia.

1 Indonesian entrepreneurship

Origins, conceptualisation and practice

Vanessa Ratten

Introduction

A vast body of research exists on entrepreneurship in North America and Europe, which has influenced the way entrepreneurship is conceptualised and studied (Adobor, 2020). This has meant most theories and conceptualisations of entrepreneurship are premised on a developed country context. Entrepreneurship occurs in different ways so it is important to consider other contexts. The stereotype of entrepreneurship occurring in only developed economies is not true as it also occurs in emerging economies. Thus, in the past decade, there has been a flurry of interest in entrepreneurship in other contexts particularly in Asia. This has led to the growth of studies on Asian entrepreneurship. However, most of these studies focus on countries such as China and India so there has been limited interest in entrepreneurship in other Asian countries. This book seeks to remedy this by focusing on the Indonesian context, thereby offering a novel and new perspective on how entrepreneurship develops based on regional, cultural and economic activity.

Entrepreneurship research in Indonesia presents a rich research domain by offering exciting research opportunities and the possibility of creating new theory (Anggadwita, Ramadani, Alamanda, Ratten, & Hashani, 2017). Indonesian entrepreneurship involves the creation and development of new ventures by Indonesian people or people with a connection to Indonesia. This can involve public, private, non-profit entities or a combination of all. The outcomes of Indonesian entrepreneurship can extend beyond Indonesia, as globally much interesting work on Indonesia is emerging. This growing body of literature is classified as "Indonesian entrepreneurship" and may include other geographic areas.

Indonesian entrepreneurship as a topic will continue to be a popular focus of study. More researchers in Indonesia and globally will shift their attention to studying entrepreneurship. This is due to the concept of Indonesian entrepreneurship attracting the attention of political and academic authorities and also to the way entrepreneurship contributes to regional development and economic growth. Researchers need to better understand what drives success in Indonesian entrepreneurship. Success is based on subjective assessments of business activity so it must consider cultural factors. This means that it can include the amount of

DOI: 10.4324/9781003187769-1

entrepreneurial activity taking place in a region or how entrepreneurship contributes to the social fabric of a place (Singh, Corner, & Pavlovich, 2007). As the body of literature on Indonesian entrepreneurship develops, it is helpful to identify challenges for the future (Patria, Usmanij, & Ratten, 2019). These challenges are based on the emerging body of knowledge on Indonesian entrepreneurship that is still developing. As research on Indonesian entrepreneurship is still in its nascent stage, its underpinnings remain based on traditional entrepreneurship theory (Erista, Andadari, Usmanij, & Ratten, 2020).

This book responds to calls to advance the entrepreneurship field by looking at new contexts. By focusing on Indonesia, it extends our current knowledge on Asian entrepreneurship by focusing more specifically at the country-level context. Currently whilst there is much anecdotal evidence about entrepreneurship in Indonesia, the English written work on this topic is sparse. This means that the conditions and timing are right for a book on Indonesian entrepreneurship. Indonesia offers unique opportunities for new insights into entrepreneurship to emerge. Most existing entrepreneurship research is biased in terms of assuming a free market economy and similar cultural conditions (Ratten, 2014a). This is not always true as there is great diversity in entrepreneurship practices.

This chapter will provide an overview of Indonesian entrepreneurship by discussing the history and culture of the country in terms of how that affects business activity. The role of entrepreneurship in society is then discussed that highlights the need for an Indonesian understanding of entrepreneurship.

Indonesia

Indonesia is a fast-growing country with the number of people living below the poverty line having decreased in recent years (Tajeddini, Ratten, & Denisa, 2017). This has led to an increase in the middle class and a booming economy. The main ethnic groups in Indonesia are the Javanese, Sundanese, Madura and Malay. Indonesia is the world's largest Islamic state although it is a secular state. Indonesia is located in the Indian and Pacific oceans. It is on the equator so it has a warm climate for most of the year. The main island of Indonesia is Java, on which its capital Jakarta is located. Previously Indonesia was called the Dutch East Indies when it was under Dutch rule. Indonesia was occupied by the Japanese during World War II then granted its independence from the Netherlands in 1945. Indonesia includes a biodiversity unparalleled in other parts of the world. Many of the islands are on tectonic plates and subject to volcanic activity. This results in a diverse environment with a close proximity to the sea. Indonesia is the largest country in Southeast Asia and has a tropical temperate. It shares a border with Papua New Guinea and Malaysia. Many of the islands in Indonesia due to their small size or location are uninhabited.

The rapidly transforming economy of Indonesia has kick-started an emphasis on entrepreneurship. This has led to more people adopting an entrepreneurial mindset with regards to business ventures. In addition, Indonesia has continued to implement ambitious market reform, thereby further fuelling its economic growth rate. This has lifted their economy and increased the standard of living for many of its citizens.

The Indonesian economy has undergone a transformation in recent years with more open trade and investment policies. Moreover, the growing middle class has led to an increase in domestic consumption. Indonesia has a younger population than other countries with a significant percentage of people under the age of thirty years old. This has led to an increase in the percentage of people in the workforce. In addition, there are strong intra-regional and international trade flows in Indonesia. The more well-known tourist destinations in Indonesia are Bali, Lombok and Komodo. However, most of the business and governmental activities reside on the main island of Java. The main economic sector is the manufacturing sector including the chemical, textiles and transportation industries. The agricultural sector is also important in terms of farming, fishery, forestry and plantation. The mining and hospitality sectors also comprise a large percentage of the overall gross domestic product. Indonesia in recent years has been amongst the world's best performing economies, and this is expected to continue in the future. Indonesia is a relationship-driven market with business relationships based on trust. This means that social networks are key to successfully doing business in Indonesia.

Indonesia consists of five main islands: Java, Sumatra, Kalimantan, Sulawesi and Papua as well as many smaller islands. Indonesia is the largest archipelago in the world and includes more than 17,000 islands. This is in distinct contrast to other countries that normally have one large connected landmass. As an archipelago, the sea is important as it provides a way to travel between islands. Indonesia is positioned between two oceans: the Indian and Pacific. Most of the land in Indonesia is mountaineous and in a sub-tropical climate. The Indonesian climate includes a wet northwest monsoon that occurs between December and March then a dry east monsoon from June to September. The warm climate impacts the type of business activity practised in the country. There is a large percentage of land covered in forest that means in many places there is fertile soil. The high volume of rainfall means there is an abundance of land for farming. Indonesia has an interesting history with the arrival of Hindu kingdoms, Indian Buddhists and Muslim traders. The Dutch occupation of Indonesia lasted more than 300 years and influenced the development of the country. Many of Indonesia's laws and regulations are still based on Dutch law.

Indonesia is amongst the most populous countries in the world, but the population distribution is highly concentrated on the main island of Java. At the heart of Indonesia's culture is the traditional decision-making rule called 'musyawarah dan mufakat', which means mutual agreement and solidarity. The Indonesian state philosophy is called the 'pancasila', which refers to the five principal beliefs of one supreme God, humanity, unity, democracy and social justice.

Entrepreneurship

There is no consensus about how to define entrepreneurship, but most definitions imply that there needs to be innovation, proactiveness and risk taking involved

(Assudani, 2009). This means that entrepreneurship in any context means doing something new related to a business activity (Ferreira, Fernandes, & Ratten, 2017). Entrepreneurship is normally not only considered as a positive activity due to the way it promotes job growth but can also be considered in a negative context as it encourages risk-taking activity. Woodfield et al. (2017: 123) define an entrepreneur as "someone who undertakes a project with assumed risk and an economic outcome". This means an entrepreneur differs from a business person due to the way they engage in business activity based on a degree of risk (Ferreira, Ratten, & Dana, 2017). Entrepreneurship is defined as "a set of personality traits (such as, for example, need for achievement, locus of control, risk-taking propensity, creativity) that, influenced by external variables (such as level of education, tenure, age, previous experiences, institutional and socio-economic factors) show the attitude of a person toward the good governance and management of a firm" (Gordini & Rancati, 2015: 172). This definition highlights the personality traits of entrepreneurs and the role of environmental contexts.

Entrepreneurship is based on perceptions in terms of how an entrepreneur carries out their activities. A key characteristic of an entrepreneur is their willingness to engage in risk. This means that they pursue business opportunities that have uncertain outcomes. Therefore, an entrepreneur not only is perseverant but also has a sense of independence in their business life. This means that they tolerate ambiguity and are able to identify opportunities. There is much diversity amongst entrepreneurs in terms of their psychological profile to the type of entrepreneurship they are engaged in. This means that there is not a general way to describe an entrepreneur as it rather depends on the context. Entrepreneurs can differ based on gender, location and level of activity. Historically much research assumed entrepreneurs to be men but this has changed with the emergence of research on women entrepreneurship. Entrepreneurship studies have tended to be based on developed country locations but this too has changed with increased interest in emerging markets. Entrepreneurship can be corporate-based or the prerogative of small business owners. This means entrepreneurship can vary from sporadic activity to continual and lengthened forms of business development.

Entrepreneurship is a dynamic process that involves creating value. To do this, business opportunities are exploited through innovative action. Entrepreneurs are a catalytic agent of change as they enable new business models to emerge in the global economy. Entrepreneurs have a number of personality traits such as a willingness to persevere despite hardship and a sense of independence that distinguishes them from non-entrepreneurs. This means entrepreneurs may be regarded as organisers that pursue innovation. They initiate action through a decisive mindset that enables ideas to progress in the marketplace. Effective entrepreneurs are needed in all contexts but particularly in emerging economies that are undergoing rapid industrialisation.

There is always some kind of risk involved in entrepreneurship but its nature in terms of impact can vary (Ratten & Ferreira, 2017). This means that financial risk is different from environmental or social risk. With any form of entrepreneurship, the future is uncertain and cannot be predicted. This means that there are fluctuating environmental factors that need to be taken into account. Innovation in business activity differentiates an entrepreneur from a manager.

Research into entrepreneurship has tended to focus on success instead of failure. This emphasis is surprising given the high failure rate for many entrepreneurs and the inherent risk involved in entrepreneurship. Failure is a stressful life event that has implications for future activity. Individuals learn from failure so for most entrepreneur's success comes after many trials and errors. Entrepreneurs often have to adapt their initial idea to suit market conditions. This means the initial envisioned opportunity changes as a result of market feedback. The word 'failure' has different connotations depending on the context. In some cultures, failure is treated as a badge of honour and is viewed as a learning opportunity. In other cultures, it is considered more in a negative context as it impacts on future behaviour. In a business setting, failure can have a small affect or more substantial affect depending on the circumstances. This means small failures can more easily be overcome whereas large failures in terms of bankruptcy or insolvency take time to adjust. Failure generally refers to some kind of deviation to the original results. This means that the desired outcome is not achieved. Singh et al. (2016) suggest that the two main recovery strategies involving the grief process in entrepreneurship are loss-oriented and restoration-orientation. The loss-oriented strategy involves taking practical steps to recover. This can involve thinking about ways to utilise unused resources in other endeavours. The restoration-oriented strategy involves avoiding thinking about the failure and instead focusing on other activities. When entrepreneurs fail, they can experience financial, psychological and social costs (Omorede, in press). As a result of failure, an entrepreneur gains new insights and information that can help them success in the future. Firm failure involves the cessation of a business because it has been deemed unsuitable. This normally means the business has not met performance expectations in terms of financial outcomes. Failure can occur for a variety of reasons including not meeting profit expectations or new technologies emerging in the marketplace. Entrepreneurs who suffer failure may face stigmatisation that leads to psychological damage. These negative emotions can be hard to overcome especially when the failure has hurt the brand image of an entrepreneurs.

Matherne, Bendickson, Santos and Taylor (2020: 990) state that an individual's entrepreneurial personal theory "defines how he/she views entrepreneurship and entrepreneurial opportunity, arising through active learning from relationships and experiences". This means an individual evaluates entrepreneurship based on how they perceive its impact. The impact is shaped by the individual's involvement in other environmental contexts. For entrepreneurs, their involvement and understanding of market trends are important. Entrepreneurs use different processes to make sense of opportunities. Sensemaking in terms of attributing meaning to experiences enables entrepreneurs to identify gaps in the marketplace. Table 1.1 illustrates the main environmental effects on entrepreneurship in terms of institutions, market structure, firm-specific and country advantages and international strategies.

Table 1.1 Major environmental effects on Indonesian entrepreneurship

Types	Examples
Institutions	Regulatory and political • free trade agreements Tax incentives Access to markets Political structure Rule of law Informal norms Political leadership
Market structure	Formal structure • trade policies • collaborative agreements Informal structure • trust systems • family-based networks
Firm-specific and country advantages	Weather and location Knowledge creation hubs Distribution of industry Dependence on technology for social interaction
International strategies	Supply chain networks Foreign direct investment

Emerging market entrepreneurship

Entrepreneurship is an independent field of research with its own theories. Thus, there needs to be a distinction between entrepreneurship in different country contexts in order to derive a better understand. This has meant that research on entrepreneurship in emerging markets has grown quickly due to interest in business activity. Most of the foundations of entrepreneurship theory derive from mature economy contexts with few studies on emerging markets (Jones, Klapper, Ratten, & Fayolle, 2018). This means that there is a reluctance of scholars and practitioners to base assumptions on existing entrepreneurship theory due to untested emerging market contexts (Ratten, 2014b). Emerging economies are different from mature markets due to their political and cultural background. This means that there is a need for more studies to focus on emerging markets due to their unique contexts. The study of emerging markets is an impactful research stream. During the past decade, there has been a fundamental change in the international business world with countries including China and India experiencing rapid economic growth. Other emerging market countries including Indonesia are also set to experience growth in the next decade. Thus, the evolution of the entrepreneurship field needs to be cognisant of this change (Ratten, Costa, & Bogers, 2019).

There have been key milestones in the emergence of emerging economies in the entrepreneurship literature particularly around how they are perceived in the literature. The main milestone has come from the realisation that emerging economies need to be studied differently to developed countries. Their history and social significance in the global economy means they have unique features. Therefore, rather than stereotyping all emerging countries as the same, they instead need to be studied as separate entities.

Networks and relationships are important for entrepreneurship as they enable resources to be acquired. In emerging economies, the social conditions mean there is an emphasis on relationships. This embeds harmony amongst individuals in a community. Human connections are necessary for any economy but are particularly relevant for entrepreneurs in emerging markets. This is due to human interaction fostering business activity. Entrepreneurship has a historical setting that is evident in the way individuals conduct business transactions.

The mainstream entrepreneurship research has neglected specific countries notably those in emerging economies. This gap seems to have narrowed in the last couple of years with the increased emphasis on new country contexts. As a result, new and diverse phenomena especially in emerging economies are being emphasised. The identification and evaluation of entrepreneurial opportunities are different in emerging economies. Entrepreneurship does not occur in the same way in emerging economies as developed countries due to the additional cultural and social differences. This means entrepreneurship should be considered not just at one point in time but also occurring at multiple intervals over a longer time period. Thus, entrepreneurial behaviour can fluctuate based on market conditions. Entrepreneurship drives market growth and normally takes the form of new business activity or the creation of additional business markets. Entrepreneurial activity provides opportunities that are not normally available in an existing market environment. This leads to the development of new innovations in the business process.

Emerging markets are defined as "low income, rapid-growth countries using economic liberalisation as their primary engine of growth" (Hoskisson, Eden, Lau, & Wright, 2000: 249). Not all developing countries are characterised as emerging markets as their economic and social growth rate has not changed. This means emerging markets are distinctive as the living standards of inhabitants are increasing and there is a new middle class. However, in emerging markets, the lack of infrastructure in terms of roads and internet access can represent a barrier to entrepreneurship.

Research on entrepreneurship in emerging economies is uncommon. There seems to be no significant difference between an Indonesian entrepreneur and an entrepreneur from another country. Rather, like all entrepreneurs, their experience and access to resources are important. However, in Indonesia, there exists a distinct business and social climate that is more conducive to entrepreneurship than that existing in other countries. There has long been a debate in the entrepreneurship literature about the role of context in influencing entrepreneurial behaviour. This arises from a practical need to know how to encourage further entrepreneurial networks.

8 Vanessa Ratten

Entrepreneurship in Indonesia

Entrepreneurship can help resolve social and environmental challenges. The literature on Indonesian entrepreneurship is still relatively sparse compared to research on other country contexts. Entrepreneurship is a field of study within the social sciences and has largely developed from anthropology, psychology, regional development and sociology studies. A complete definition of Indonesian entrepreneurship may never be agreed upon due to the multitude of factors inherent in its conceptualisation.

The concept of Indonesian entrepreneurship has several interrelated facets. It is not just about business ventures, but it also involves opportunity discovery. This means the process can be synthesised into different aspects based on environmental factors. We live in a world of digitalisation where increasingly most of the business transactions are conducted partially or fully online. This has shaped how we communicate with others and led to a digital-based culture. Until recently, most of the scholarly work on entrepreneurship has focused on motivations or reasons for individuals to behave in an innovative way rather than understanding the context that makes an individual pursue entrepreneurial opportunities. This book proposes that Indonesia represents a unique and valid context for studying entrepreneurship.

Entrepreneurship has always been an integral part of the Indonesian economy, a fact made evident by the number of new business ventures being established in the country. However, the amount and degree of entrepreneurship evident in Indonesia are obscured sometimes by the lack of research on the topic. This makes the complex mechanisms behind entrepreneurship in Indonesia difficult to understand. Entrepreneurship in Indonesia must be analysed separately from other country contexts. Indonesia is undergoing rapid change making it necessary to study the multifaceted business environment. In recent years, firms in Indonesia have been forced to adapt to new challenges including changes in consumer habits and living conditions. Therefore, the adaptation behaviour of Indonesian consumers has resulted in a growing interest in entrepreneurship. Entrepreneurs have been looking for new strategies in order to respond to market needs and develop alternative income-generating activities. Entrepreneurs are individuals who aim to maximise profits by identifying market gaps. The relationship between an entrepreneur and their market environment is a complex subject, since the entrepreneur can be a manager, owner or licensee depending on the circumstances. The methods used to analyse entrepreneurship in Indonesia can be transferred from existing research in other country contexts. However, when studying Indonesian entrepreneurship, its specificities should be considered including climatic conditions and political temperament.

The entrepreneurship existing in Indonesia mainly not only comprises a large number of small businesses but also occurs in large business contexts. Entrepreneurs play a crucial role in the Indonesian economy since they are the ones who start and develop new businesses. The specific cultural context of Indonesia makes it an interesting country to study the configuration of entrepreneurial resources. Moreover, the impact of entrepreneurship on the environment, land-use and landscape is different. This means the role of entrepreneurship is not only to produce economic gain but also to create cultural change through monetary pursuits. Research on Indonesian entrepreneurship can be evaluated in terms of its cultural identity and institutional structure. Culturally, the historical evolution of Indonesia as a republic and independent nation needs to be considered in terms of its impact on entrepreneurship. This means understanding how historic events helped shape and influence entrepreneurship. In addition, the institutional structure of the Indonesian economy means entrepreneurship is developed in a different way. This means that the religious and community underpinning of entrepreneurship needs to be understood.

Considering the incongruities in the literature on Indonesian entrepreneurship, the objective of this chapter is to better comprehend its evolution in recent years. Entrepreneurship in Indonesia is diverse due to the variety of business activity conducted in the region. It is interesting to study the collective passion of Indonesian entrepreneurs that continually evolve based on new market conditions becoming evident in society. Entrepreneurs possess certain skills and traits that differentiate them from non-entrepreneurs. In times of social upheaval, entrepreneurs have a tolerance for risk and ambiguity that enables them to quickly respond to change.

Research on Indonesian entrepreneurship to date is dwarfed by the amount of research on North America and Europe. Researchers thus know very little about Indonesian entrepreneurship or the way entrepreneurs in Indonesia differ from other country contexts. This remains the case despite the fast growth of the Indonesian economy and its emphasis on entrepreneurship. Research on Indonesian entrepreneurship represents an important contribution towards understanding how country context influences entrepreneurship, thereby highlighting the benefits of a more global approach to entrepreneurship scholarship.

Indonesian entrepreneurship is sufficiently distinguished from mainstream entrepreneurship to argue that is a sub-field of research in its own right. There are two main perspectives in the entrepreneurship literature: the emergence and opportunity school of thought. The emergence perspective views entrepreneurship as a dynamic process that evolves over time. This means individuals acquire ideas about entrepreneurial endeavours that put these thoughts into action. This process does not necessarily follow any specific path as it depends on the passion and perseverance of the entrepreneur. The opportunity perspective is more well known than the emergence perspective because it has been emphasised in recent entrepreneurship literature. The opportunity perspective focuses on how ideas are discovered, evaluated then exploited in the marketplace. Ideas can be discovered in a variety of different ways including through experience or interaction with others. Once ideas are discovered then they need to be evaluated in terms of market potential. This can involve feasibility studies to understand the resource requirements. The exploitation stage then involves commercialising the idea in order to ensure its profitability in the marketplace.

Indonesian entrepreneurship involves the discovery and exploitation of business opportunities in Indonesia. This involves creating new markets by evaluating current business trends. Scholars and practitioners who study Indonesia from an entrepreneurial perspective are studying Indonesian entrepreneurship. The domain of Indonesian entrepreneurship includes both new and existing business activities. It can involve any type of entrepreneurship ranging from the more industrialised view of entrepreneurship to emerging forms of digital innovation. Entrepreneurship is a multifaceted phenomenon as there are many ways business activities can be innovative, risk taking and proactive. Therefore, Indonesian entrepreneurship accommodates many different perspectives. The rise of Indonesian entrepreneurship is connected to the culture, history and religious conditions in the country.

Indonesian entrepreneurship: levels of analysis

To fully understand Indonesian entrepreneurship, the role of different levels of analysis from the individual, organisation and network perspective needs to be acknowledged. Individual entrepreneurs have different motivations for organisations and those in network relationships. Therefore, each unit of analysis should be analysed in order to differentiate how the country's context influences their performance.

Individual level

Individuals and small groups of traders are essential to the entrepreneurial spirit of Indonesia. Enterprising individuals establish new firms or grow existing firms. They can be small business owners or gig economy entrepreneurs depending on the business context. Entrepreneurs play a key role in rejuvenating regions and areas in order to facilitate new business activity. Entrepreneurs are in charge of exploring business opportunities and make a contribution to the economic development of a region. Indonesian entrepreneurship has a strong cultural element in terms of the way business ideas emerge in the community. Thus, Indonesian culture plays an important part in business life and influences entrepreneurial activity. Cultural institutions including the church, school and government influence the type and number of entrepreneurs in society. Indonesian entrepreneurs can use their culture in business endeavours. This means integrating cultural values in business.

Organisational level

There is a long tradition of entrepreneurship in Indonesia. This is due to the emphasis on trading between the islands that comprise Indonesia. Moreover, within each island of Indonesia, there is a culture of entrepreneurship that is related to the local customs and traditions. The current research on Indonesian entrepreneurship is sparse and from an English language perspective virtually non-existent. Whilst there may be a lot of research on Indonesian entrepreneurship written in Bahasa Indonesian, the predominance of English language journals and books means that it is not widely read. In order to rectify this anomaly, more research on Indonesian entrepreneurship written in English will help to grow interest in the field. Entrepreneurship is a dynamic field as it constantly adapts to suit market conditions faced by organisations. Thus, there has been an increased recognition of the vibrancy and relevance of entrepreneurship in Indonesia. It is necessary to focus on organisational level phenomena in Indonesia as it is agenda setting in terms of discussing future research trajections involving Indonesian entrepreneurship. Indonesian entrepreneurship is complex with respect to understanding what exactly constitutes entrepreneurship.

Network level

Research on entrepreneurship from different country contexts is increasing in prevalence but there remains a lack of focus on emerging economies such as Indonesia. It is important to consider Indonesian approaches to entrepreneurship as it influences the relevance of entrepreneurship research and the comparability of findings across countries. Uncertainty is a key characteristic of entrepreneurship that is lessened through network relationships. The outcomes of entrepreneurial activity are not always known and often depend on luck. Failure can be a precursor to success as it enables an entrepreneur to start again more intelligently. At this point, we know very little about Indonesian entrepreneurship. Focusing on the Indonesian context, there needs to be more emphasis on network relationships.

Goal of this book

This book on Indonesian entrepreneurship offers a comprehensive account of the state of the art in the area of entrepreneurship and Indonesia. In doing so, it focuses on the transformation of the Indonesian economy to a more entrepreneurial-based society. It sets the fundamental principles of entrepreneurship by offering ideas and guidance for the road ahead. This includes offering a wide range of contributions from the area of entrepreneurship including service design, technological innovation, business management, data analytics, resilience and innovation mapping. Each of these topics is discussed from an entrepreneurship perspective and explored in different ways.

The material covered in this book derives from research and practice, thereby denoting scientific relevance with practical implications. As the book is strongly based on practice, it has significant practical value by presenting real-world applications. This enables cutting-edge innovations to be discussed that highlight the relevance of entrepreneurs in Indonesia. This book comes out at a time when entrepreneurship is being used as a way to solve societal problems arising from the Covid-19 pandemic. Currently the global economy is centred on trying to overcome the Covid-19 pandemic through a process of vaccination. This has meant that many entrepreneurial policies are centred around Covid-19-related issues. The preliminary analysis in Indonesia indicates that entrepreneurship is increasingly apparent in business and society. Therefore, entrepreneurship acts as a source of recovery and a light for future innovations. The Covid-19 pandemic has impacted digitalisation and forced businesses to break with the past and imagine new possibilities. The ethos of this book is that supporting entrepreneurship with new ideas and a positive perspective will solve economic and social problems. This will help businesses create solutions that can be rapidly integrated into the market.

Conclusion

This chapter has discussed the importance of studying entrepreneurship from an Indonesian perspective, thereby offering a novel view about the role of culture and history in the development of an entrepreneurial culture. The role of context in terms of geographical and social linkage to Indonesia was discussed in terms of entrepreneurship. This enabled a theory of Indonesian entrepreneurship to be built that also links with practice.

References

Adobor, H. (2020). Entrepreneurial failure in agribusiness: Evidence from an emerging economy. *Journal of Small Business & Enterprise Development*, 27(2), 237–258.

Anggadwita, G., Ramadani, V., Alamanda, D. T., Ratten, V., & Hashani, M. (2017). Entrepreneurial intentions from an Islamic perspective: A study of Muslim entrepreneurs in Indonesia. *International Journal of Entrepreneurship and Small Business*, 31(2), 165–179.

Assudani, R. (2009). Ethnic entrepreneurship: The distinct role of ties. *Journal of Small Business & Entrepreneurship*, 22(2), 197–205.

Erista, I. F. S., Andadari, R. K., Usmanij, P. A., & Ratten, V. (2020). The influence of entrepreneurship orientation on firm performance: A case study of the Salatiga Food Industry, Indonesia. In *Entrepreneurship as empowerment: Knowledge spillovers and entrepreneurial ecosystems*. Bingley, United Kingdom: Emerald Publishing Limited.

Ferreira, J. J., Fernandes, C. I., & Ratten, V. (2017). Entrepreneurship, innovation and competitiveness: What is the connection? *International Journal of Business and Globalisation*, 18(1), 73–95.

Ferreira, J. J., Ratten, V., & Dana, L. P. (2017). Knowledge spillover-based strategic entrepreneurship. *International Entrepreneurship and Management Journal*, 13(1), 161–167.

Gordini, N., & Rancati, E. (2015). Entrepreneurship and growth of small family firms: Evidence from a sample of the artistic craftsmen of Florence. *Sinergie: Italian Journal of Management*, 33(98), 169–194.

Hoskisson, R., Eden, L., Lau, C., & Wright, M. (2000). Strategy in emerging economies. *Academy of Management Journal*, 43(3), 249–267.

Jones, P., Klapper, R., Ratten, V., & Fayolle, A. (2018). Emerging themes in entrepreneurial behaviours, identities and contexts. *The International Journal of Entrepreneurship and Innovation*, 19(4), 233–236.

Matherne, C., Bendickson, J., Santos, S., & Taylor, E. (2020). Making sense of entrepreneurial intent: A look at gender and entrepreneurial personal theory. *International Journal of Entrepreneurial Behaviour & Research*, 26(5), 989–1009.

Omorede, A. (in press). Managing crisis: A qualitative lens of the aftermath of entrepreneurial failure. *International Entrepreneurship and Management Journal*, pp. 1–28.

Patria, D., Usmanij, P. A., & Ratten, V. (2019). Survivability and sustainability of traditional industry in the twenty-first century: A case of Indonesian traditional furniture SME in Jepara. In *Subsistence entrepreneurship* (pp. 131–153). Cham: Springer.

Ratten, V. (2014a). Encouraging collaborative entrepreneurship in developing countries: The current challenges and a research agenda. *Journal of Entrepreneurship in Emerging Economies*, 6(3), 298–308.

Ratten, V. (2014b). Future research directions for collective entrepreneurship in developing countries: A small and medium-sized enterprise perspective. *International Journal of Entrepreneurship and Small Business*, 22(2), 266–274.

Ratten, V., Costa, C., & Bogers, M. (2019). Artisan, cultural and tourism entrepreneurship. *International Journal of Entrepreneurial Behavior & Research*, 25(4), 582–591.

Ratten, V., & Ferreira, J. J. (2017). Future research directions for cultural entrepreneurship and regional development. *International Journal of Entrepreneurship and Innovation Management*, 21(3), 163–169.

Singh, S., Corner, P., & Pavlovich, K. (2007). Coping with entrepreneurial failure. *Journal of Management & Organization*, 13, 331–344.

Singh, S., Corner, P., & Pavlovich, K. (2016). Spirituality and entrepreneurial failure. *Journal of Management, Spirituality & Religion*, 13(1), 24–49.

Tajeddini, K., Ratten, V., & Denisa, M. (2017). Female tourism entrepreneurs in Bali, Indonesia. *Journal of Hospitality and Tourism Management*, 31, 52–58.

Woodfield, P., Woodfield, P., Woods, C., Woods, C., Shepherd, D., & Shepherd, D. (2017). Sustainable entrepreneurship: Another avenue for family business scholarship? *Journal of Family Business Management*, 7(1), 122–132.

2 Artisan entrepreneurship in Indonesia

Vanessa Ratten

Introduction

The craft industry preserves cultural traditions through connecting artistic endeavours to economic gains. It does this by combining new and old elements by linking historical processes to current artistic endeavours. This means that the craft industry provides job and business opportunities that contribute to the economic development of a region. Each artisan product is hard to replicate due to the time and skills involved. This means that the key feature of artisan products is that they are made to high-quality standards. To do this takes a skilled craftsperson who has had experience or training in the production methods.

Artisans are responsible for the entire process of designing a product to actually producing a product. Artisan businesses are small scale and are the opposite of large-scale industrial producers. This means that artisans focus on quality and a desire to make something that is culturally significant to society. This involves thinking about the production process in a way that produces a unique product. Artisan entrepreneurship is not limited to specific crafts as it can occur in a wide variety of contexts. The word 'artisan' is similar to 'craftmanship' but implies a more intricate and thought-out design process. This means it includes skills not often considered crafts such as cheesemaking but are part of cultural production. Thus, artisans make a variety of products from cheese, coffee and bread to chocolate and fashion. Moreover, the term 'artisan' implies some kind of design process in which the aesthetic is important. This means craftmanship whilst being very similar to artisanal activity implies a lower level of design activity.

Arias and Cruz (2019: 633) define artisanal enterprises as making "products made either completely by hand, or with the help of hand tools or even mechanical means, as long as the direct manual contribution of the artisan remains the most substantial component of the finished product". Artisan products provide a link between the place-bound features of a region and the preference to consumer local products. Increasingly authentic and rare products are preferred by consumers particularly those who visit a region as a tourist.

Artisanship is often a lifetime project and interest for those involved. This means the traditions and culture are associated with the skill mastery of an artisan. Arias and Cruz (2019: 634) define artisanship as "an individual occupation,

DOI: 10.4324/9781003187769-2

a social position within communities and a lifestyle career that included apprenticeship, several years of travelling and practice to master a craft, and the establishment of a stable, independent enterprise". This means it can take a long time to be considered an artisan due to the effort required to learn the trade.

Only recently has more attention from an academic standpoint been given to artisan entrepreneurship. Whilst the practical significance of artisan entrepreneurship to regional development has been known for some time, academic research particularly from an entrepreneurship point of view has been slower to gain momentum. The aim of this chapter is to look more closely at the process of artisan entrepreneurship in order to bridge the gap between practice and academic scholarship. This means focusing on the aspects and conditions that make artisan entrepreneurship unique compared to other forms of entrepreneurship.

The creative economy is known for its entrepreneurship that is evident not only in products but also in the type of business ventures that proliferate in the sector. There is also a high degree of labour market fragmentation in creative businesses. This means there are many self-employed or gig workers that differentiate the sector from other industries. Considering the socio-economic and cultural significance of artisan businesses a detailed insight into their entrepreneurial activity is required. This will provide valuable advice for how artisan entrepreneurs operate in society and how policymakers can encourage further growth. Moreover, such insights into artisan entrepreneurship can inform business support policies and lead to more value creation. Artisan entrepreneurship is a label given to craft or handicraft business ventures. This label refers to the cultural and heritage element endemic in any artisan entrepreneur. Artisan entrepreneurs create products by hand or are supported by tools. Therefore, this chapter focuses on answering these research questions, which are divided into the following sub-questions:

1 How has artisan entrepreneurship changed over time?
2 What is the role of artisan entrepreneurs in community development?
3 How has artisan entrepreneurship changed based on certain environmental contexts?

The creative industries

In the past decade, the role of creative industries has grown in the global economy. Creative industries refer to businesses that have their economic activity derived from a creative pursuit (Bakas, Duxbury, & De Castro, 2018). This includes entertainment and leisure activities that are based on creativity. The creative economy is gaining increased global recognition as an important driver of social and economic growth (Chandra & Salimath, in press). Within the creative economy, many individuals are self-employed and follow a lifestyle business model. This has meant that the creative economy is a leading driver of employment, innovation and economic growth. Summatavet and Raudsaar (2015: 31) define the creative industries as "an economic sector based on individual and collective creativity, skills and talent and the ability to create welfare and jobs through creating and using intellectual property". Entrepreneurship is a key trait of the creative industries in terms of establishing, maintaining then growing artisan businesses. There are a range of businesses that can be considered as artisan including art, design, information technology, music, performing arts and publishing. Artisan businesses are highly diverse in nature with each one being unique. This means that it is important to study each artisan business on a case-by-case basis rather than making stereotypical assumptions.

Craft and artisan entrepreneurs operate in the creative industry, thereby mostly focusing on handmade items (Hill, 2020). Many craft entrepreneurs learn their skills through cultural connections that are passed down generations (Fillis, 2006). By creating tangible products, artisans often personalise their work. This means although most of the work is handmade, there is also support from machines or technology. Artisans create small batches of products that are notable for their individual style (Hoyte, 2019). This is in contrast to mass-produced goods that are not individually produced. This means that many artisan products are unique and this characteristic differentiates them in the marketplace (Igwe, Madichie, & Newbery, 2019). Artisan entrepreneurs can be found in the brewing, food, glass work and pottery work. There has been a resurgence of interest in artisan entrepreneurship due to more attention being placed on handmade goods (Marques, Santos, Ratten, & Barros, 2019). Individuals have more time for handicrafts and this has led to a growth in the craft industry. An example of a handicraft industry is batik, which is discussed in the next section.

Batik in Indonesia

Batik is a centuries-old technique of hand-dyeing cloth with patterns made from wax. Many people in Indonesia wear batik on a daily basis and it is considered a part of the culture. Batik is on the UNESCO cultural heritage list because of its special relevance in Indonesian culture. Batik is continually evolving and adapting to suit new societal needs. Batik is made by applying a penlink tool or stamp dipped in wax. This process is repeated many times in order to create complex patterns.

Batik has made a resurgence in contemporary clothing and housewear. It comes from the Island of Java where the technique originated from. The use of batik can be traced back to the ancient Egypt and Tang dynasty in China. It came to prominence in the 19th century in Indonesia. To make batik, patterns are created by pouring hot wax onto undyed fabric. The fabric is then dyed and the wax removed in order to show the patterns.

The process is then repeated with different colours or designs. The making of batik is considered an artisan technique due to the knowledge required to make the produce. Artisan batik makers use cantings, which are copper devices that look like fountain pens to make patterns on fabric. They pour the wax very precisely and utilise traditional techniques to make the patterns. Some artisans also use wood blocks or other devices to make patterns.

The patterns on the batik denote different symbols or stories. Many patterns are designed for visual appeal and their perceived beauty. Other patterns have special meanings and can only be worn by certain individuals. This includes the parang pattern that has knife-like symbols that only royals can wear. To use a canting takes a high level of skill and practice. The canting can have different sized sprouts used to make various shapes. The wajan is the container used to hold the melted wax. Normally it is made of iron or earthenware and placed on a stove in order to keep the wax in a melted state. It is important that the wax is kept at a specific temperature as if it is too hot it will spread too quickly and if it is too cold it will clog the canting. Artisans often blow onto the wax on the canting in order to cool it before applying it on the cloth.

The use of a canting to make patterns is a time-consuming process as it requires specific skills. The wax for batik can be beeswax or paraffin. The cap or copper stamp is made to use specific designs on the fabric. Each cap is made from copper strips into certain shapes. The dyes used in the making of batik primarily consist of black, brown, blue and beige colours. Traditionally the colours were made from plants and from natural ingredients. Artisans draw an outline of the pattern onto the cloth before applying the wax. These designs can be created by hand or traced from stencils. In order to apply the wax, artisans sit on a low stool or mat. The fabric is placed over bamboo frames called gawangan in order to allow the wax to dry. As mistakes are difficult to correct, artisans need to be experienced when they apply the wax. After the wax has been applied, it is then placed into earthenware tubs to be dyed. To make deeper colours the fabric is left in the tub for a longer time period. To make new colours, the fabric is dyed again and the wax reapplied. Normally batik has different colours so it is placed into the tub multiple times. Batik designs are associated with religious ceremonies and traditional festivals. There are certain batik designs used in weddings.

The ceplok design is a series of geometric patterns based on circles, squares or stars. It can also include flower or animal pictures. The design creates an illusion of depth in the fabric. The kawang design consists of intersecting circles. This design is also used on temples. Modern batik artisans are using new pictures and designs. This includes the use of flowers and birds. Artisans no longer have to use natural dyes so are incorporating new colours. Traditionally batik was sold in lengths used to make traditional sarongs. This has changed with different sized fabrics being made available in order to use on tablecloths and other home furnishings.

The craft industry

McAuley and Fillis (2005: 139) state that the craft industry is part of the cultural industry and includes "designer trades, book publishing, the music industry, television and radio broadcasting, independent film and video, the art trade and cinema". This means there are a range of contexts in which the craft industry operates in society. These contexts involve varying degrees of entrepreneurial activity that can take time to develop. The creative industries have traditionally been considered as one of the most innovative industries due to the high level of artistic expression. Within the craft industry exist a number of different types of artisans who are involved in creating new products. The cultural industries are linked to the culture and history existing in a region. This means embedded in each cultural product is some form of heritage or tradition.

Craftspeople are central to the cultural and social fabric of Indonesia. They have protected the cultural heritage by promoting the arts and crafts industry (Fillis, 2010a). Craftspeople have endured despite the mass production of certain items becoming popular. They offer a way to keep traditions by focusing on historical and cultural significance in products. This enables cultural identities to persist. Artisans differ from industrial producers due to the high level of manual skill involved (Fillis, 2010b). This means that most of the products are handmade and take more time to produce than industrial products. The decorations in terms of colour and design are also specific to artisan goods. This means that they are identifiable not only by their design but also by the linkage to cultural traditions. An artisan product is characterised by the way it is made (Kuhn & Galloway, 2015). Indonesia has a long tradition of artisan entrepreneurship. Most of these small firms are in the art, clothing and textile industry. Craftspeople have a high level of creativity due to the way they design and source material.

People produce craft goods for financial, personal and social needs. The income received from craft work often comes in the form of cash. This means it is linked to the informal economy that is based on cash-based transactions. The word 'craft' refers to some form of activity that takes an artistic nature. This means that it involves special skills that require time to develop. Craftmanship refers to custom-made goods that are constructed in high-quality ways. Artisans employ craft-based methods and manual techniques to make products. The craft-based methods can include embroidery or knitting to make clothes or use handmade techniques to make food. This means there are manual techniques in the design and production process. Artisan goods are normally made in small batches and take time to produce. Artisan goods embody a high level of quality in the way they are produced.

The concept of artisan entrepreneurship involves craft-based business activity. This means the artisan whilst involved in craft activity also makes the product for financial or social gain. Normally the monetary incentive outweighs the societal contribution of making the artisan product. Artisan products can be made via the application of skill-based knowledge. This results in small-scale production methods that emphasise thought in the entire production process. Industrial production processes make products in a large volume without individualising each product. Artisans whilst in the past did everything by hand now also sometimes use machines. This makes the difference between artisan and industrial production resides in the thought process towards the product. Therefore, artisan products have a set of values that emphasise quality and design. Industrial products differ by emphasising large-scale production that results in quickly made products that are of low quality.

Artisans often have a desire to make something without thought for the outcome. This makes them focus on the task at hand in a thought-out way, thereby the work is done by unifying the head and hand. Artisans are not associated with any specific craft but rather are concerned with skilled production methods. The work of artisans can refer to chocolate making to fashion goods. Artisans often utilise traditions and practices associated with rural cultures. This ensures the heritage of a region is maintained whilst making products through artistic expression. This can make the process slow and time consuming. However, the resulting product is made with effort and novelty. The products artisans make need to be fluid and relative to cultural traditions. This means they bridge the past with the present in terms of incorporating new design processes with cultural ideas. Artisan products are socially constructed based on aesthetic and symbolic values. This makes them distinct from ordinary goods that have a more functional meaning. Artisan products bring the idea of craft through handiwork to the surface. This makes the handiwork being part of the aesthetic nature of a product. Artisans have a distinct philosophical approach to their production methods as they try to incorporate cultural ideas. This means utilising traditional craft methods rather than technological-based production. The main motivation for an artisan is the artistic expression rather than a commercial need. This means the artisans identity is typically tied to the product. Artisan entrepreneurs simultaneously play the role of artist and business person. The most significant characteristics of artisan entrepreneurs involve the skill and craft that goes into the design and production process. This means emphasising provenance and aesthetics in each product.

Artisan entrepreneurship

An artisan is a skilled craftmaker that creates products or services by hand. Artisans learn through experience and their skills are often tied to tradition. Skills processed by artisans are learnt based on their desire to create individualised products. This means that as compared to mass-produced goods, artisan-made products are unique. Whilst some products can appear similar in design, each product will have different features. The term 'artisan' refers to an artist skilled at making things by hand. This means there is a degree of creativity expressed in each product. Artisans take pride in their work as they are conscious of the quality of each product (Sawyer, 2000). This means artisans normally have a high level of social consciousness in terms of how the products they are making are perceived in the community (Tregear, 2005). This means there is a sense of social obligation to the communities in which they reside in order to preserve the culture and tradition.

Artisans typically use simple and non-technology-related devices to make products (Taylor & Littleton, 2008). This includes painting implements, scissors or carving to make decorative objects. Artisan products can be both functional and/or aesthetic. Artisans produce things with their hands without using machines. The word 'artisan' also refers to crafting and handcrafts. Many crafts have been practised for centuries and artisans use the same techniques. Artisans can use traditional material such as wood that has been in existence for a long time or can recycle new material. In some artisan products, there is a cultural or religious significance. The industrial revolution decreased the significance of craftspeople in the economy. This meant there was a decrease in people making things by hand due to the introduction of machinery. With the advent of the knowledge economy, there has also been a change to more computer-orientated crafts, but there are also many people still preferring handmade products.

Crowley (2019: 261) refers to artisan entrepreneurship as "the marketing of creative assets in which manual techniques take precedence". Artisan entrepreneurs produce products that have a strong link with a specific place or culture. This means that the craftmanship is associated with cultural practices. This differentiates artisan products from mass-produced goods. Entrepreneurial behaviour is evident at the micro, macro and meso level in artisans. At the micro level, the focus is on how the individual artisan is entrepreneurial. This means understanding the reasons for entrepreneurship and the way cultural factors influence innovative behaviour. At the macro level, the focus is on how economic or regional factors influence artisan entrepreneurship. Some regions might support artisans more than others due to their impact on economic development. This is related to the way artisan communities encourage tourism. At the meso level, it focuses on societal factors influencing artisan entrepreneurship. In times of crisis such as that occurring during the Covid-19 pandemic, people have had more time to spend on handicrafts. This has led to a surge in interest on artisan entrepreneurship. Artisan entrepreneurs are normally tied to a specific location due to cultural or social factors (Pret & Cogan, 2019). This means that artisans use locally available resources in order to make their products. Depending on the type of product the resources might only exist in a certain place and not be available anywhere else. Artisan entrepreneurs value their independence and unique way of making products. Artisan entrepreneurs differ from commercial entrepreneurs as they place a high emphasis on personal well-being (Ratten, Costa, & Bogers, 2019). This difference is a critical factor explaining the growth in artisan entrepreneurship. In addition, there has been an emphasis on emotional well-being so artisan entrepreneurship might relate to this topic (Ratten & Ferreira, 2017). The balance between work and life aspects is becoming more important in entrepreneurial decisions. Table 2.1 depicts the framework for Indonesian entrepreneurship research in terms of key themes and outcomes.

Artisan entrepreneurs play a crucial role in maintaining the cultural heritage of an area. This facilitates economic and social development whilst preserving the cultural conditions in an area. Entrepreneurship in general is viewed as a source of innovation and growth. This means that artisan entrepreneurs provide a source of growth that then has spillover effects to other areas of the economy. Artisan entrepreneurs in recent years have flourished by focusing on craft-based initiatives. There has been a growing international awareness of cultural issues which has led to increased demand for artisan products. Artisan products are viewed as authentic and a way of providing a cultural connection.

Table 2.1 Framework for Indonesian artisan entrepreneurship research

Research approach	View of artisan entrepreneurship	Key themes	Main outcomes
Sociology	Systematic cultural practice that encourages artistic expression in business practices	Cultural and social management	Cultural and social change
Artistic and cultural challenges	Innovative solutions to cultural problems	Co-creation and collaboration	Socio-cultural development
Artisan development	Satisfying artistic needs through financial gain	Development of relationships between artisans and consumers	Cultural, social and community cohesion

Artisan entrepreneurs find ways to turn their hobbies into sustainable businesses. This means normally artisan businesses are lifestyle-based and tied to an individual's passion. Unlike other types of entrepreneurs who might focus on profitability, artisan entrepreneurs also seek to integrate prosocial practices into their business models. This means there is a sense of civic duty in their business dealings that differentiates them from traditional entrepreneurs.

Artisan entrepreneurs are normally small businesses operating at the local level. With the advent of the internet, these businesses have been able to set up relatively cheap websites to internationalise their business activities. This has led to a community of like-minded artisans advertising their services online. Artisan entrepreneurs are not often motivated by a quick profit due to the time it takes them to make each product. Rather they are motivated by the enjoyment they receive from the production of the product. Artisans can be classified as lifestyle entrepreneurs as they are interested in business activities that are conducive to their way of life. To be classified as an artisan entrepreneur, the mission of the business needs to be artistic in nature and includes handmade activities. This means the economic value creation is seen as a side product rather than the sole reason or the business. In addition, artisan entrepreneurship is characterised by hybrid elements of both cultural and financial motivations. This means that the label of artisan refers to someone who is making a product with traditional methods. The process of making the product has a historical element as it normally has occurred over a long time period. Moreover, the complexity of the combination of cultural heritage with modern-day artistic elements makes artisan entrepreneurship unique.

Folklore and local heritage form part of artisan entrepreneurship. They provide a valuable source of inspiration for the creation of artisan products. Entrepreneurship as a concept has tended to focus more on large-scale corporate ventures rather than artistic endeavours. This has meant the growth in interest in artisan entrepreneurship is a relatively recent phenomenon that has coincided with more interest in the cultural and creative industries. Artisan entrepreneurs are driven by cultural, social and economic reasons. Thus, artisan entrepreneurs have tended to pursue a low or non-growth orientation as they are content with their current business activity. Artisans are a special type of entrepreneurs as they are more focused on cultural-based business ventures. This means they focus on the production and sale of handmade goods that are tied to the cultural aspects of a region. Furthermore, artisans practice certain forms of trade that involve manual techniques. Although, more recently, these manual techniques can be supplemented by the use of computer-aided techniques. This means there is a great deal of diversity in terms of how artisans make and market their products.

Artisanal knowledge is proprietary and often location dependent. This means that the knowledge embedded in an artisan is of a specific nature that takes time to acquire. The skills an artisan has are the result of traditional production methods. To acquire this knowledge, artisans learn by doing or through training processes. This makes personal judgement a key part of an artisan's skill, thereby creating an intimate connection between handmade activity and thought processes. In addition, the knowledge an artisan has can be embedded within a local pattern of interaction. This makes artisans acquire knowledge through intuitive connections with their crafts. This makes the knowledge an artisan has be based on first-hand experience and social interaction.

Artisans individualise their products in subtle ways. Artisan businesses continue to prosper despite widespread industrial production of goods. This is due to the associated cultural link with artisan products. Whilst many artisans produce products for financial gain, there is also a growing number of artisans who produce products as a voluntary or leisure-time activity. Some artisans have reinvented themselves in order to produce alternative and individualised products. This creates economic and cultural value to society.

Artistic orientation of entrepreneurs

Purnomo (2020: 1) defines artistic orientation as "the individual desire to make artistic contributions in the form of original artwork or journalism, or in arts studies". This means that individuals who are more artistic tend to promote freedom of expression in their endeavours. This enables them to expand their art into new and innovative areas. Artisan entrepreneurs tend to have some form of artistic orientation due to them being in the creative industry. Artisans need to consider both economic and artistic logic in their endeavours. Economic logic is apparent when profit-seeking motives are integrated into the production of artisan products. Artistic logic is evident when aesthetic concerns are paramount in the design of products. This involves artisan products that have a high level of beauty. Feelings in the form of emotions are part of the creative process. Every artisan is affected by the way they feel when making their products. Positive emotions are likely to be beneficial for the production of artisan products, whereas negative emotions might harm or delay the process. Artists are conscious of how their emotions can be transferred into making products. Art refers to the process and the resulting product stemming from the creative activity. Purnomo (2020: 4) describes art as "the conscious use of skill and creative imagination especially in the production of aesthetic object". To make art normally some form of expression is evident in the activity. This can include artistic movement in dance, drawing on paper or using a chisel to carve patterns. There is some degree of subjectivity in art as individuals consider some expression as art whereas others regard it as normal activity. Moreover, traditional art can differ from modern art so there also needs to be consideration of time and history in the decision.

Artistic expression is an essential part of society and is increasingly being used in a business context. Products or services that embed an artistic spirit are valued in society. This is due to the time and care taken to make them. Unlike mass-produced products, artisan products are differentiated by the time and effort required to make them. This means consideration is given to the ingredients or materials needed for their production. In an increasingly competitive marketplace, it is important for products to have a niche market appeal. Consumers are becoming more discerning about the types of products they buy. This is influencing a trend towards artisan products. Artisan products not only are made by hand but also are unique in terms of their marketability. This means that they are valued by consumers in the marketplace.

Many artisans exist at subsistence or poverty levels, but there are also lifestyle artisans who have a higher standard of living. This means there are many different types of artisans that can be distinguished based on their living conditions. In emerging markets, artisans make products for survival reasons. This also happens in developed countries, but there is also a trend towards opportunity entrepreneurs who make artisan products because of their interest in these products. Artisans are socially important in communities as they contribute to the social fabric of society. They maintain traditions whilst teaching others culturally valuable skills. Artistic expression is embodied in the culture and history of a region. Artisans employ craft-based skills that require time to acquire. Typically, this involves hand stitching or handmade material that is used in the production process.

Artisans should use an agile business model in terms of constantly improving their products based on new knowledge acquired. This involves experimentation with ideas that result in better quality. Marketing agility is defined as "a firm's strategic means for executing growth activities by the marketing organization and its members through simplified structures and processes, fast decision-making, and trial and error learning" (Homburg, Theel, & Hohenberg, 2020: 10). This definition emphasises agility in a marketing sense is a complex and ongoing activity involving different areas of a firm. To succeed in the global marketplace, being agile is a valued firm trait. Kalaignanam, Tuli, Kushwaha, Lee, & Gal (2020: 36) define marketing agility as "the extent to which an entity rapidly iterates between making sense of the market and executing marketing decisions to adapt to the market". Within this definition is an emphasis on iteration in terms of obtaining feedback then improving the process. This enables a firm to adapt to new conditions by making sense of changing environmental conditions. Kalaignanam et al. (2020) suggest that marketing agility incorporates four main concepts: sensemaking, iteration, speed and marketing decisions. Sensemaking involves understanding information that is available. To do this requires reducing confusion by analysing its core meaning. Due to unexpected events in the marketplace, it is important to understand new developments. This can be hard to do due to the existence of ambiguity. Therefore, it helps to establish a shared understanding of the vent in order to make sense of what has happened. Iteration involves making changes based on feedback and suggestions. This enables ideas to be refined in order to perfect the idea. Before making decisions it helps to analyse the potential impact. This involves recognising the risks involved then trying to minimise the impact. Thus, a firm can pivot and change based on developing events.

Speed involves how quickly an enterprise can adapt to the marketplace. Artisan businesses need to be flexible in their market approach due to the way business is changing. The time taken to assess market changes then to initiate action is important. Fast decision-making based on the knowledge available is needed. This ensures that businesses can adjust to the market environment in the right way. Marketing decisions involve making rapid adjustments to a firm's strategy. This involves obtaining the best results and benefits from a marketing campaign.

Social networks amongst artisan entrepreneurs

Artisans are socially embedded in their community as they rely on social ties for business activity. The social connections an artisan has enable them to overcome liabilities of newness when growing their business. This means the social context can help an artisan entrepreneur connect with like-minded people. This can facilitate market interaction and lead to more business opportunities. Artisans need the social creativity that is derived from being a member of an entrepreneurial ecosystem. This enables creative ideas to continue to flow in society and makes it easier for artisan entrepreneurs to enter the marketplace. Creativity can take time to develop and often needs to be fostered through social interaction.

Networks enable a range of participants to surpass normal boundaries in order to cooperate. The connectedness in a network fosters the sharing of information. This gives rise to new opportunities and increases innovation. Information amongst network members is diffused through the sharing of knowledge. This form of knowledge transfer enables ideas to progress and the overall firm performance to increase. Not all information shared in a network system is positive as it can also constrain the activity of network members. This means knowledge needs to be evaluated in terms of how it can be used to commercialise new ideas.

Networks are helpful in overcoming resource deficiencies. This enables firms to stay competitive by utilising their network relationships. Networks are defined as "an infinite set of formal and informal relationships that lead to collaborative actions between persons, groups, communities, organisations and governments" (Kokkranikal & Morrison, 2011: 139). Due to rapid technological change and empowered customers, there is a need for artisans to utilise their networks to facilitate better market transactions. These networks enable firms to leverage resources and human capital in a way that is not possible by themselves.

Social networks provide a useful way of understanding the connections amongst individuals in a group. Social networks are defined as "a specific set of linkages among a defined set of persons, with the additional property that the characteristics of these linkages as a whole may be used to interpret the social behaviour of the persons involved" (Baggio & Cooper, 2010: 1758). Within a social network, there are a number of stakeholders that enable it to function. These stakeholders refer to individuals or entities that matter. More specifically, a stakeholder is defined as "any person, group or institution that has an interest in a development activity, project or program" (Baggio & Cooper, 2010: 1759). Stakeholders have a vested interest in discussions about economic growth. This means they are normally included in any decision-making process. Stakeholders are affected by the objectives of a region and influence its performance. Increasingly stakeholders due to their legitimate interest in discussions are called activists. This means their participation is a means of increasing the overall effectiveness of a region. Not all stakeholders are equal as they vary in size. This means each stakeholder needs to be considered in terms of their role in a network. A well-formed social network enables stakeholders to have more input through a process of value creation.

Cavallo, Ghezzi and Sanasi (in press: 4) define a value network as "any web of relationships generating tangible and intangible value based on complex dynamic exchanges between two or more network participants such as individuals, groups or organisations". Not all networks are positive as there are power dynamics existing. This means more powerful players in a network can obtain more value than less powerful entities. Therefore, each network relationship needs to be evaluated based on the level of interaction that leads to value creation. The value might not be immediately known as it can take time for entities to transform ideas into business ventures. This means it is helpful to view entrepreneurial ecosystems as complex and messy due to the non-linear path they often take in the marketplace. Initial collaboration paths for entities in an entrepreneurial ecosystem may diverge due to competing interests. This means that an ecosystem can be viewed as a living system that constantly changes. Value can be negotiated amongst entities in an ecosystem based on need. This is due to value often being subjective and dependent on the need of the business entity.

Artisan entrepreneurship research can be analysed in terms of three major levels of analysis: firm, industry and community. At the firm level, it concerns individual artisans and how they behave in an entrepreneurial manner. The focus is on the individual or firm involved in the artisan activity. Analysing specific characteristics of individual artisans can help to understand their motivations for engaging in business activity. Moreover, it helps to understand the socio-demographic influences of artisan entrepreneurship. This includes the age, gender and location of an entrepreneur. The industry level focuses more at the industry effects of artisan entrepreneurship. This includes whether the artisan business is in the tourism, health or retail industry. There are different industry effects in terms of intensity of competition that influence artisan activity. For artisan businesses located in rural areas, the location might lead to associations with tourism. This means it is useful to analyse the entrepreneurial ecosystems associated with an artisan in terms of understanding the related effects of other stakeholders. This includes government officials, other businesses, regulatory authorities and research institutions. Each of these stakeholders will contribute in their own way to the level of entrepreneurial activity in a region. As artisan businesses often involve collaboration with non-profit or government agencies, it can also be useful to use an entrepreneurial ecosystem analogy to understand the effects. The community level focuses on the societal influences of artisan entrepreneurship. Due to the Covid-19 pandemic, people have spent more time at home. This has led to an increase in handicrafts and home-based hobbies.

Handicraft industry

Handicrafts are sometimes viewed as a hobby or folk art although for many they are also a source of income. Handicrafts require specialised knowledge and hours of training. This can include highly technical information that needs specialised facilities for production. Handicrafts can be perceived as being useful or art objects depending on the context. Increasingly people are learning handicraft skills for pleasure rather than for purely financial reasons.

The explosion of interest in artisan products has coincided with the Covid-19 crisis. More people working at home has meant for many more time to pursue home-based crafts. Moreover, individuals in the tourism and hospitality sectors have filled their time by focusing on creative pursuits due to lockdown and working restrictions. At the same time, individuals are more interested in nostalgic and homemade items that have a cultural link. This has led to an increase in hobby-based artisan businesses that enable individuals to earn money whilst pursuing a hobby. During the Covid-19 crisis, more artisans are selling their products online. This has opened up new marketing and selling channels that were previously not considered. The artisan economy has been praised as a way to combine cultural pursuits with financial gain. This is viewed as a sustainable and ethical business strategy as compared to mass industrialisation practices. The artisan economy enables more localised and community-minded economic activity.

There are various types of artisans including those who view their business as more of a hobby rather than a source of financial income. These hobby entrepreneurs have increased during the Covid-19 crisis because they have spent more time indoors and at home on craft activities. Other types of artisans include those who are more business minded and rely on their business as their main source of income. These include artisan food producers who create specialist food such as cheese or honey. There has been an increase in interest by consumers about knowing where and how their food has been grown. This makes it important for artisan food producers to highlight the authentic nature of their product. There are many different types of handicrafts such as food, home goods, paper goods, wood and textile making, which are stated in Table 2.2.

Table 2.2 Types of Indonesian handicrafts

Type of material	Examples
Food	Cake making, egg decorating, cheese making
Home goods	Basket making, candle making, quilting, soapmaking
Paper goods	Bookbinding, card binding, origami, paper-mache, stamping, scrapbooking
Wood, metal, clay, glass, stone goods	Carpentry dollhouse, enamelling, glassblowing, jewellery, puppet making, sculpture, stained glass, toy making, word carving
Textile making	Banner making, batik, cross-stitch, crochet, embroidery, knitting, lace making, embossing leather, macrame, needlepoint, rug making, saddle art, silkscreening, tapestry, t-shirt art

Artisanal food

Lindbergh and Schwartz (2021: 150) state that "artisanal food is produced on a small scale, usually grown and harvested locally, and emphasises tradition, authenticity and craftmanship in both production and flavour". This means, unlike mass-produced food, artisan food is carefully made in line with cultural considerations. Therefore, it connects food to culture in a way that is not evident in other forms of food production. In addition, the emphasis on tradition ensures that the food is similar to that made by previous generations. This continuity in culture is a key feature of artisan food and the reason for its popularity. Moreover, the craftmanship ensures that quality considerations in terms of taste are considered.

Local food systems can be complex due to the need to make products in an efficient way whilst maintaining quality. As a result, there are competing logics of commercial ability and authenticity that are challenging to manage. Such competing logics create tension in artisan entrepreneurs' everyday activities. Artisan food is sold in a variety of settings including farmers markets, supermarkets and online stores. However, the increased interest in farmers markets has made artisan food more popular. This has coincided with food trends such as local and organic farming methods. The number of artisans in the economy is increasing due to more people becoming interested in the craft industry. Artisans are motivated by creative pursuits that do not involve complex technology. This means their production methods are normally basic but can involve a high level of skill.

Arias and Cruz (2019: 636) state that artisanal chocolate production "can be comprehensive (e.g. growing, processing and transforming cacoa beans into chocolate products) or partial (e.g. acquiring processed cacoa beans to artfully create diverse chocolate confections". Popular artisan food products include confectionery such as chocolate. Artisan-made chocolate is handmade with locally distinct ingredients. Increasingly artisan chocolate is being appreciated due to the difficulty in the production methods. This is because of the mastery of production techniques needed to make artisan chocolate.

Craft beer

There has been a rise in interest in craft beer due to its varied brewing techniques and new flavours. This has led to more independent breweries developing to cater for this growing market. Whilst traditional artisan brewing has existed for a long time, recently there has been a resurgence in interest. The quantity produced by craft beer manufacturers is typically low with their products having more of a creative appeal. Craft beer reflects the desire to create niche products that are reflective of cultural practices. This means the ingredients in craft beer tend to be made from more natural or herbal ingredients. In addition, craft breweries have a more flexible approach to the way beer is made. This enables them to be able to experiment with new flavours and tastes. The emphasis in craft beer is on quality through traditional brewing methods. Craft brewers have more unique methods of fermenting that enable them to produce a different taste. Before the introduction of large commercial breweries beer was produced at the location in which it was sold. Some craft breweries have reintroduced this practice as a way to connect with customers. The overall beer industry has grown at a fast pace over the past decade. In conjunction with this trend has been craft breweries that differentiate their products based on unique tastes. The vast majority of craft breweries tend to be micro-businesses that employ a small number of people. This is due to some craft brewers being interested in brewing more as a hobby rather than as a purely commercial endeavour. This means that entrepreneurs establish a craft beer business due to their enthusiasm. As a result, craft beer produced is not standardised but subject to individualised outcomes. Craft brewers tend to use new ingredients or recipes to further differentiate their products. The popularity of craft beer has led to them being acquired by large breweries.

Jamu

Jamu is a traditional herbal medicine popular in Indonesia. Its ingredients are normally sold in bottles and include natural materials such as flowers, honey, leaves and fruit. It is recognised as one of Indonesia's intangible cultural heritage as it represents a cultural practice prevalent in Indonesia. Jamu is most prevalent in Java where Javanese women travel house to house selling herbal medicines. Often Jamu is sold on the street as a drink sweetened with honey or sugar. More recently, it is sold in stores in satchel packaging that requires water before drinking. Jamu medicine varies from region to region and is often not written down but passed down generations through verbal communication. Due to the abundance of herbs and spices in Indonesia, there has been a strong interest in Jamu. The increasingly health-conscious middle-income bracket has influenced the increase in domestic sales.

Jamu drinks are typically made with turmeric and ginger. Jamu as a traditional herbal medicine has been practised for centuries in order to treat disease and maintain health. Despite the increased usage of conventional medicine treatments, Jamu is still very popular. Indonesia has a high number of indigenous medicinal plants that can be used in traditional herbal medicines. Jamu means traditional medicine from plants. Jamu gendong are freshly prepared jamu sold in warungs. A warung is a small business existing in Indonesia that is part of everyday life. Many warungs are family owned and operate from a room in a family's home. Warungs refer to small neighbourhood convenience stores. There are different kinds of warung from those selling local food snacks to other daily necessities. Warung kopi are coffee shops that also serve a social function. Warung jamu are stores that sell traditional herbal medicine.

There has been an increase in more larger scale and modern production methods to make jamu. Jamu is based on traditional knowledge and experience making it an integral part of the Indonesian healthcare system. Jamu is an inherent part of Indonesian culture and is a long-standing cultural tradition. During the Covid-19 pandemic, the demand for jamu has increased due to people wanting to boost their immune system. In Indonesia, most of the jamu sellers are women.

Conclusions

This chapter has sought to answer the following question: What is the role of artisan entrepreneurs in the global economy? To answer this question requires reflective thinking about how artisan entrepreneurs differ to other types of entrepreneurs. I close this chapter with three main observations about artisan entrepreneurship. The first concerns the research trajectory of artisan entrepreneurship. In moving the field of entrepreneurship forward, it is important that future research takes new paths. This means emphasising creativity in thinking about new topics like artisan entrepreneurship. I urge researchers and practitioners to reflect on how they conceptualise and measure artisan entrepreneurship. This will help to develop new conceptual work based on theory that can be empirically tested.

The second observation is on placing more emphasis on theory development about artisan entrepreneurship from different contexts. Theory-building efforts are important in developing a new research effort. This means that a theory of artisan entrepreneurship can be derived based on existing literature from the creative industries and entrepreneurship fields. A broad spectrum of literature can then be consulted on in terms of developing a comprehensive definition of artisan entrepreneurship. Artisan entrepreneurs may differ based on industry structure and geographic location. Thus, a new theory that starts with an existing theory that is then applied to an artisan environment may provide useful results. There should be some academic freedom in developing theory related to artisan entrepreneurship. This will enable new practices to emerge that is consistent with real-life experience.

The final observation is about the critical role of conceptual development. Entrepreneurship as an academic field is relatively new compared to other fields such as economics and sociology. This means that, in order to progress knowledge, there should be new concepts emerging in the literature. Conceptual contributions about artisan entrepreneurship will contribute to entrepreneurship research and thought. This will help motivate others to research artisan entrepreneurship because of the prospect of generating exciting ideas.

References

Arias, R. A. C., & Cruz, A. D. (2019). Rethinking artisan entrepreneurship in a small island: A tale of two chocolatiers in Roatan, Honduras. *International Journal of Entrepreneurial Behavior & Research*, 25(4), 633–651.

Baggio, R., & Cooper, C. (2010). Knowledge transfer in a tourism destination: The effects of a network structure. *The Service Industries Journal*, 30(10), 1757–1771.

Bakas, F. E., Duxbury, N., & de Castro, T. V. (2018). Creative tourism: Catalysing artisan entrepreneur networks in rural Portugal. *International Journal of Entrepreneurial Behavior & Research*, 25(4), 731–752.

Cavallo, A., Ghezzi, A., & Sanasi, S. (in press). Assessing entrepreneurial ecosystems through a strategic value network approach: Evidence from the San Francisco Area. *Journal of Small Business and Enterprise Development*.

Chandra, V., & Salimath, M. (in press). When technology shapes community in the cultural and craft industries: Understanding virtual entrepreneurship in online ecosystems. *Technovation*.

Crowley, C. (2019). Artisan entrepreneurial behaviour: A research agenda. In *Entrepreneurial behaviour* (pp. 261–280). Cham: Palgrave Macmillan.

Fillis, I. (2006). Art for art's sake or art for business sake: An exploration of artistic product orientation. *The Marketing Review*, 6(1), 29–40.

Fillis, I. (2010a). The art of the entrepreneurial marketer. *Journal of Research in Marketing and Entrepreneurship*, 12(2), 87–107.

Fillis, I. (2010b). The tension between artistic and market orientation in visual art. In D. O'Reilly & F. Kerrigan (Eds.), *Marketing the arts: A fresh approach* (pp. 31–39). Abingdon: Taylor & Francis/Routledge.

Hill, I. (2020). Spotlight on UK artisan entrepreneurs situated collaborations: Through the lens of entrepreneurial capitals and their conversions. *International Journal of Entrepreneurial Behaviour & Research*, 27(1), 99–121.

Homburg, C., Theel, M., & Hohenberg, S. (2020). Marketing excellence: Nature, measurement, and investor valuations. *Journal of Marketing*, 84(4), 1–22.

Hoyte, C. (2019). Artisan entrepreneurship: A questions of personality structure? *International Journal of Entrepreneurial Behavior & Research*, 25(4), 615–632.

Igwe, P. A., Madichie, N. O., & Newbery, R. (2019). Determinants of livelihood choices and artisanal entrepreneurship in Nigeria. *International Journal of Entrepreneurial Behavior & Research*, 25(4), 674–697.

Kalaignanam, K., Tuli, K., Kushwaha, T., Lee, L., & Gal, D. (2020). Marketing agility: Conceptualization, research propositions, and a research agenda. *Kenan Institute of Private Enterprise Research Paper No. 19-22*.

Kokkranikal, J., & Morrison, A. (2011). Community networks and sustainable livelihoods in tourism: The role of entrepreneurial innovation. *Tourism Planning & Development*, 8(2), 137–156.

Kuhn, K. M., & Galloway, T. L. (2015). With a little help from my competitors: Peer networking among artisan entrepreneurs. *Entrepreneurship Theory and Practice*, *39*(3), 571–600.

Lindbergh, J., & Schwartz, B. (2021). The paradox of being a food artisan entrepreneur: Responding to conflicting institutional logics. *Journal of Small Business and Enterprise Development*, *28*(2): 149–166.

Marques, C. S., Santos, G., Ratten, V., & Barros, A. B. (2019). Innovation as a booster of rural artisan entrepreneurship: A case study of black pottery. *International Journal of Entrepreneurial Behavior & Research*, *25*(4), 753–772.

McAuley, A., & Fillis, I. (2005). Careers and lifestyles of craft makers in the 21st century. *Cultural Trends*, *14*(2), 139–156.

Pret, T., & Cogan, A. (2019). Artisan entrepreneurship: A systematic literature review and research agenda. *International Journal of Entrepreneurial Behavior & Research*, *25*(4), 592–614.

Purnomo, B. R. (2020). Artistic orientation in creative industries: Conceptualization and scale development. *Journal of Small Business & Entrepreneurship*, 1–43.

Ratten, V., Costa, C., & Bogers, M. (2019). Artisan, cultural and tourism entrepreneurship. *International Journal of Entrepreneurial Behavior & Research*, *25*(4), 582–591.

Ratten, V., & Ferreira, J. (2017). Future research direction for cultural entrepreneurship and regional innovation. *International Journal of Entrepreneurship and Innovation*, *21*(3), 163–169.

Sawyer, R. K. (2000). Improvisation and the creative process: Dewey, Collingwood, and the aesthetics of spontaneity. *The Journal of Aesthetics and Art Criticism*, *58*(2), 149–161.

Summatavet, K., & Raudsaar, M. (2015). Cultural heritage and entrepreneurship – Inspiration for novel ventures creation. *Journal of Enterprising Communities: People and Places in the Global Economy*, *9*(1), 31–44.

Taylor, S., & Littleton, K. (2008). Art work or money: Conflicts in the construction of a creative identity. *The Sociological Review*, *56*(2), 275–292.

Tregear, A. (2005). Lifestyle growth or community involvement? The balance of goals of artisan food producers. *Entrepreneurship & Regional Development*, *17*(1), 1–15.

3 Food artisan entrepreneurship in Indonesia

Vanessa Ratten

Introduction

The culture of Indonesia is a result of its rich history and interaction with other societies. This means there are art, furniture and cultural events associated with its traditions. Many cultural events are associated with folklore (Jones, Klapper, Ratten, & Fayolle, 2018). Indonesians have a strong tradition of preserving their cultural heritage through the production of handicrafts and food. This tradition has been linked to the customs and culture existing in a region. Despite the industrial revolution and increased emphasis on modernisation, there is still a strong interest in the production of handicrafts (Ratten, 2014). The centuries-old artistic legacy is preserved in Indonesia through the making and selling of artisan goods. Indonesia is known for its artisanry in its products due to the artistic and creativeness of its people. There are many artisan products in Indonesia that are made by craftsmen and women who have a desire to keep cultural traditions alive whilst making a financial income.

Indonesia is a country located in Southeast Asia that has a large population but relatively small landmass. Indonesia is amongst the largest producers of handicrafts. This includes carved figures, placemats and other decorative objects. It has a rich heritage of making artisan products. Artisans have evolved and changed in the past decade but still keep the same production methods (Santos, Marques, Ferreira, Gerry, & Ratten, 2017). Their marketing and sales techniques have altered to keep up to date with digital technology. Artisan-made products are a way of life in Indonesia and a way of integrating craft with business pursuits (Santos, Marques, & Ratten, 2019).

This chapter provides three theoretical contributions to the artisan entrepreneurship literature. First, it is amongst the first to embed an entrepreneurial passion perspective, thereby connecting the artisan literature to a new stream of research. Artisans are inherently passionate as many pursue their craft because it is a hobby. This means passion is evident in the way they structure and manage their business. Second, it contributes to an emerging line of literature on artisans and the entrepreneurial process. This means focusing on the way artisans develop their business based on emerging environmental conditions. Third, this chapter makes a contribution to the literature on entrepreneurial identity by adding a

DOI: 10.4324/9781003187769-3

creative perspective. This enables more focus on how creative individuals such as artists and craftmakers pursue entrepreneurship.

Artisan production

An attempt at defining the word 'artisan' is made difficult due to the lack of academic research on the topic (Phillipov, 2016). The word is commonly used in practice to refer to a person making a handmade product using cultural elements. This means an artisan is a small-scale producer whose intuitive judgement enables a product to be made (Milanesi, 2018). Thus, there is a high degree of skill and knowledge in the production process. Unlike manufactured products that use mechanised and automated methods, an artisan individually makes each product. This results in care and attention placed in the making of each product.

Artisans produce products that not only incorporate cultural and historical elements in their products but they can also include intangible cultural elements such as folkstories and myths. Culture is a complex and highly social phenomenon that influences society. The idea of authenticity is important to artisans as it influences the reputation of their products. Consumers are searching for more authentic and genuine products. Authenticity is a subjective notion that depends on an individual's perception about its meaning. Thus, an artisan product can be viewed as being authentic based on an individual's social conditioning. Traditional crafts have played a crucial role in defining a region to the rest of the world. Cities and towns are known for their crafts, and people travel to these regions because of the brand name recognition (Ferreira, Fernandes, & Ratten, 2017). Despite their increased usage of information technology, many regions retain a strong craft identity. Artisans often viewed commercialisation as undermining their reputation and image in the marketplace. This led to conservative growth strategies of an unplanned nature. The origin of artisan products is in the authentic use of production methods. This means that a simple process is used to create products. Artisans use their skills to make products in a unique way, and this can include aesthetic pleasing designs that are culturally distinct or functional designs based on usefulness.

Artisan production is a form of creative expression and serves as a source of income for many people. Craftwork enables a person to work in a cultural industry, thereby providing a source of economic and cultural benefit. Artisans normally have a preference for making unbranded and personalised products. Although sometimes these products are branded to show their authenticity, there is a sense of simplicity in artisan products although the process to make them can be quite complex. Artisan products are characterised by their locality and transparency. The locality refers to where the product is made and how culture traditions have influenced the production process (Ferreira, Ratten, & Dana, 2017). The transparency refers to the openness of what materials and processes were used to make the product. Therefore, provenance does matter in artisan goods as it determines how they were made and produced.

Consumers often buy artisan products because of their link to a culture or region. This means they are willing to pay a higher price for a product that is made in a specific region or by a special technique. Artisans are sometimes considered as hobbyists who charge lower prices due to them not being as financially motivated as other producers. This means they are artisans as a hobby and have other ways to produce an income. There are increasing numbers of artisans who are hobbyists due to their interest in work/life balance. This means they forego profit maximisation in return for being involved in the making of artisan products. They are not concerned with the quantity of goods sold but rather interested in artisanry as a hobby. The next section will discuss in more detail the role of food in Indonesian culture.

Indonesian food

There is a great deal of variety in the food found in Indonesia. This stems from Indonesia's colonial, immigrant and indigenous history. Indonesian food is rich in spices, and rice is the staple food for most of the people. A famous Indonesian condiment is sambal, which is a paste made from various spices. In Indonesia, there are rumah makan (eating houses) that are informal restaurants. In addition, there are many warung, which are street stores. Nasi goreng (fried rice) is a popular dish as well as gado gado (vegetables with peanut sauce).

Indonesian culture is focused on the community with the national motto being Bhinneka Tunggal Ika, which means unity in diversity. It is mentioned in the constitution of Indonesia and is considered a way of life. This emphasis on diversity is evident in the wide range of foods available in Indonesia. Indonesians believe in the concept of gotong royong, which means mutual assistance. Therefore, there is a strong emphasis on collaboration in business activities.

There is much regional variation in food in Indonesia due to the existence of different ethnic groups. Most of the meals in Indonesia consist of two main dishes and a broth or soup. The main dishes are served with rice or noodles in a traditional way. Many meals are also served in a communal way. There are different kinds of ceremonies and rituals linked to food activities in Indonesia. The tropical fruits in existence in Indonesia include durian, which are spiky, smelly fruit. Rambutans which are red fruit covered in soft spices are also popular. Belingbang (star fruit) are common as they have a cool and crisp taste. Jambu air (water apple) is a pink bell-shaped fruit that is often served as a side dish or dessert.

As the majority of Indonesians are Muslim, eating kolak (fruit in coconut milk) after the Ramadan festival is popular. Lesser Eid or Lebaran marks the end of Ramadan. During this time, festive meals and social gatherings are popular. During this time, ketupat (rice in packets of woven coconut) are consumed. Lebaran is a national holiday in Indonesia and lasts for two days. On the day of lebaran after morning prayers, people will greet others by saying 'selamat idul fitri' (Happy Eid). Families will normally also have special food on this day. Idul Adha or festival of sacrifice is celebrated after lebaran. During this time, a sheep or goat is sacrificed and the meat is shared amongst family and friends. In Bali that has a majority Hindu population, food is used for symbolic reasons. This means rice in woven banana leaf packets are placed where a god or spirit may reside.

Art and artisanship

Artisan products have a human element and a sense of art. Chakrabarti (2020: 135) states that "art is innately multifarious and embodied in people, communities, cultures and histories". Art is a universal concept that has expressive properties. This means art is a way of communicating to others through design. Art is subjective so it refers to any kind of activity that shows some degree of expression. This means activities such as drawing, writing, playing music, dance, poetry, pottery and sculpture are all considered as art. Art is similar to craft but normally refers to a non-functional process, whereas craft implies a practical usage. This means a craft incorporates some kind of knowledge and skill that takes time to develop. Folk art incorporates both craft and art as it refers to cultural expression. Cultural heritage refers to "an effort to conserve not only physical objects but also intangible elements such as art, language and customs" (Chakrabarti, 2020: 137). Preserving cultural traditions is important in many societies. This means that recognising the value of historical traditions such as artisans and art makers is valued. The production of art requires some form of creativity and imagination. Thus, it can be used as a way to share information. As art can have a number of different meanings there are limitless ways to how it can be produced.

Communal approaches to art require a number of people working tougher on a project and help to build a sense of community. Artists take pride in their work in terms of its aesthetic appeal or usefulness. Art can be spiritual and have religious meanings. Therefore, care needs to be taken by those who hold strong beliefs about the meaning of art. Chakrabarti (2020) suggests that cultural identity in art can take an anthropocentric or cosmocentric point of view. The anthropocentric views humankind as being the key enabler in the universe. This means people have the most important position in society and can make societal transformations through art. The cosmocentric views the ecological environment as being the key enabler and acknowledges the interaction between humans and the natural environment.

The creative economy represents an important way to combine creative and business pursuits (Ratten & Jones, 2021). It is a global driver of economic growth and contributes to a region's competitiveness. The sector is known for its hobbyist nature with many involved in businesses that combine work and life interests. This means there is a high number of self-employed artisans or micro artisan businesses that employ a small number of people. Hobbies are activities an individual enjoys pursuing in their leisure time. They provide a sense of enjoyment and relaxation without any sense of obligation. The voluntary nature of engaging in a hobby means that it involves a sense of passion. This enables an individual to identify with a challenge then pursue it in their own time (Ratten & Usmanij, 2021).

Artisan entrepreneurs are part of the creative and craft industries. Artisan entrepreneurs differ from other types of entrepreneurs due to the way they make products through handmade processes. Hobbyist entrepreneurs pursue their passion through business pursuits. This means the initial business venture might develop more casually and in an informal manner. Hobbyist entrepreneurs tend to be involved in business as a side activity rather than full-time pursuit. This can change over time depending on how the business develops. Hobbyists create their products using ingenuity and novel ideas. This means there is a degree of experimentation involved in the development of each product. The slow process involved in making a product by a hobbyist ensures a carefully produced good. However, the long time taken to make each product can result in production delays. This means some form of adjustment or adaptation is needed when a hobbyist becomes an entrepreneur. The production of a product by a hobbyist is a passion rather than solely a financial output. Many craftspeople are part of a group or team of like-minded people. Being part of a team is useful in sharing resources and ideas. It can also enable better market opportunities to be captured through the pooling of creative abilities or talents.

Artisan entrepreneurship

Entrepreneurship is a dynamic and not static activity as it evolves over time. Rae and Carswell (2001: 152) define entrepreneurship as "the process of identifying opportunities for creating or releasing value, and of forming ventures which bring together resources to exploit those opportunities". Entrepreneurs learn through experience about how to recognise and act on opportunities. An artisan entrepreneur is a person who has a deliberate strategic intent to pursue market opportunities. This means they recognise novel opportunities in the marketplace then exploit them through the creation of business ventures. Entrepreneurship is a mindset that is used to engage in business activities. It involves creating or developing an economic activity based on innovative ideas. Each entrepreneur has their own personal characteristics and managerial strategies that are used for business purposes. The notion of entrepreneurship has changed over time due to new business activities emerging in the marketplace. The entrepreneurship literature differs between necessity (those who have to start a business because of financial reasons) and opportunity (those who choose to start a business based on perceived market gap) entrepreneurs.

A lifestyle entrepreneur is an individual who is motivated by personal needs in pursuing a business activity. This means the personal interests are more important than financial goals. Increasingly lifestyle reasons such as being independent, leading a healthy life and choosing how you spend your time are influencing entrepreneurial behaviour. Quality of life is being valued more in society. A lifestyle entrepreneur is primarily interested in obtaining enjoyment from business pursuits. This means that financial goals are not the main reason for entrepreneurship but are still an important motivator. Lifestyle entrepreneurs seek control over their life priorities through their daily activities. This means that they seek independence and improvement in their quality of life. A lifestyle entrepreneurs' business is an integral part of their life. The passion displayed by a lifestyle entrepreneur influences the aspirations they have for their business.

Lifestyle entrepreneurship is a way of living and working that is becoming increasingly popular in society. There is a cultural and social change occurring in society due to the increased emphasis placed on issues such as work/life balance, sustainability and climate change. Entrepreneurs are now expected to engage in socially responsible practices.

Artisan entrepreneurs are innovative and shape markets. Artisans may reject the notion of entrepreneurship when it is defined as a commercialisation activity but accept it when it is referred to more broadly as innovation. Artisans adopt an entrepreneurial orientation when they have to survive and adapt in the marketplace. An entrepreneurial orientation refers to a mindset that emphasises innovation in decision-making activity. The individual artisan is the key player in making entrepreneurial decisions. Innovativeness refers to the tendency to support new ideas that incorporate some degree of creativity. This means emphasising novelty and change. In order to be innovative, some experimentation is required. Proactiveness refers to actively being engaged in thinking about the future. This involves having a forward-looking perspective that anticipates change. Individuals who are proactive are able to recognise trends before they occur. This can help them gain a competitive advantage in the marketplace. Risk taking involves taking action that has an uncertain outcome. This involves a willingness to take action without a known result.

Many artisans are passionate about their craft and this is reflected in the quality of the products they produce. Passion is a key behavioural characteristic of entrepreneurs as it enables them to overcome obstacles. Hubner, Baum and Frese (2020: 1112) define entrepreneurial passion as "the consciously accessible, intense positive feeling experience by engagement with roles that are meaningful and salient to self-identity". Entrepreneurs are involved in various activities such as innovation and developing a business. Being passionate enables an entrepreneur to persist in adverse environments where the outcome is unknown. Due to the difficulty in progressing an idea in the marketplace, entrepreneurs who are passionate can persist when others may fail. This means, in stressful circumstances, passion is required in order to manage challenging circumstances.

Artisans have a distinct entrepreneurial orientation that differentiates them from other types of entrepreneurs. This is due to the creativity inherent in making an artisan product that is the result of innovative thinking. Entrepreneurial orientation is a strategic stance artisans take in the marketplace that emphasise innovation. This enables them to generate value and capture more interest in their products. Artisans are driven by their passion for their craft and satisfaction from being involved in the process of craft making. There is not only a sense of prestige from being an artisan that is associated with the way they make products but also a social appeal to artisans particularly those who live in an attractive rural location.

Social media and artisan entrepreneurship

Social media is an effective mechanism that can contribute to an artisan's marketing and strategy objectives. It enables them to involve customers more in the craft making process, thereby acting as an important source of communication. Kapoor et al. (2018: 536) define social media as "various user-driven platforms that facilitate diffusion of compelling content, dialogue, creation and communication to a broader audience". This means that it provides a source through which information can be exchanged through social interaction. It enhances two-way communication between artisans and customers, thereby enabling artisans to broadcast information to a large audience and facilitating more interactivity. Social media is an electronic service that provides a platform for sharing information. It includes social networking websites, internet forums and blogs.

Artisans have a sense of identity from engaging in their craft. Self-identity is derived from how an individual interacts with others. Identity is a continually evolving and changing based on the environmental context. Artisans are increasingly using digital media, which enables them to document and share information about their craft. Digital media enables diverse modes of communication to be developed that ensures more real-time information is made available. This enables artisans to develop their brand name and enhance interaction with customers and their community. Artisans can develop their craft knowledge by publishing updates on digital media. This enables them to obtain feedback from others in order to improve their craft. There are also unexpected benefits for artisans from engaging in digital media platforms. This includes new designs and production methods to emerge based on interaction with others. The creation of digital media context such as audio, graphics and video are valuable skills for artisans. Social media such as Facebook, Instagram and LinkedIn are important for artisans especially for those in remote locations.

Artisans can share ideas and obtain real time feedback on social media. This is an important way for global communities of practice regarding artisanship to emerge. Social media enables communication through online sources regarding a certain topic. Moreover, social media is driven by user-generated content that is constantly being updated. This has meant there is a large amount of information available on social media. Social media integrates multiple sources of media and enables different points of view to emerge. It is based on internet technologies that enable the creation and modification of content. This enables user-generated content to be exchanged as a source of information. The focus of social media is on collaboration and establishing information linkages. Social media is initiated and circulated based on the interests of users. This means that the content provides a source of information on brands, products and topical issues.

Social media is changing how artisans do business. It enables artisans to enhance brand loyalty in their interaction with audiences. Interest in artisan entrepreneurship as a distinct category of entrepreneurs has increased in recent times. Their distinctiveness is marked by the integration of cultural, historical and artistic activity. Artisan enterprises are a form of hybrid organisation as they combine economic, social and cultural logics. Hybrid organisations integrate social and market goals. This means that they often pursue competing goals.

Entrepreneur's identity

An entrepreneurial identity is an individual's perception of their belief in being an entrepreneur. This means that, someone who thinks, they have an entrepreneurial attitude can be considered as being an entrepreneur. An individual's identity serves as a way of evaluating their position in society. This means that it can be used to distinguish individuals from others based on their behavioural characteristics. More individuals are considering themselves as entrepreneurs because of the positive meaning associated with being an entrepreneur. An entrepreneur is viewed in society as being a social change agent and important contributor to economic development. This means that they pursue opportunities based on perceived market gaps. Being an entrepreneur can be an arduous task as it involves focusing simultaneously on innovative, risk taking and futuristic activity. Entrepreneurs take control of critical resources by pursuing market gaps. This involves strategic planning and anticipating demand. Lifestyle entrepreneurs construct their identity based on what values matter most to them.

An entrepreneur's identity can be examined through role and social identity theory (Żur, 2020). Role identity theory refers to the position a person has in society. This is associated with the way an individual acts and behave. It incorporates the expectations and meanings associated with a role. This means that context is an important determinant of how a role is perceived. Social identity theory relates to an individual being a member of a social group. Therefore, an individual will act in a certain way based on their position in a social group.

Artisans sometimes have scant entrepreneurial capabilities due to their interest in their craft instead of business pursuits. Suvanto, Niemi and Lähdesmäki (2020) divide entrepreneurial identity into entrepreneurial orientation and personal orientation. The entrepreneurial orientation involves behavioural traits such as innovativeness and competitiveness. This means that an individual can be characterised as being entrepreneurial when they are willing to take risks and pursue market opportunities. In addition, an entrepreneur is more persistent and optimistic than other individuals. This means that they tend to be more self-reliant and focused on intended outcomes. Personal orientation refers to an individual's belief in certain behaviour such as a willingness to change the status quo. Each individual in society is different so it is important to consider their personal characteristics. This includes understanding their personal work preferences and attitudes towards business.

An entrepreneurial identity refers to the meanings an individual associates with their entrepreneurial activity in the marketplace. Individuals have a psychological and economic need to associate with a certain identity. This includes having a social identity in society that enables them to have a sense of belonging. This enables them to be included as a member of a group. The feeling of belonging is required in society. It reduces anxiety and loneliness. Individuals generate positive emotions from their identity. This enhances their psychological health and position in society. In order to become an entrepreneur, artisans need to have an intention to start a new business. This involves thinking at some point in time to establish an artisan-based business. An entrepreneurial mindset involves consciously wanting to engage in innovative business activity. This reflects an urge to do something that involves entrepreneurship. It directs an individual's energy towards entrepreneurial behaviour.

Intentions are amongst the best way to measure actual behaviour. This means that sometimes intention is used as a proxy for actual behaviour. Pinpointing an artisan as an entrepreneur carries behavioural responsibilities. This includes actively looking at new opportunities and proactively engaging in business pursuits. Artisans acquire an entrepreneurial identity based on the environmental context. Artisans might become entrepreneurs due to the influence of their social circle (e.g. family, friends, peers). This social pressure influences them to become entrepreneurs. There is pressure to conform to the expectations of an individual's social circle. This means that an artisan can embrace more entrepreneurial activities in order to fit into their social group.

Artisan entrepreneurs often learn by doing. This means that experiential learning occurs as an entrepreneur learns through experience. Artisans continually learn and are a repository of information. This means that there are significant collaborative peer learning behaviours that occur amongst artisans. Collaborative learning enables not only individuals to increase their competence and knowledge about their craft but also artisans to share experiences and reminisce about past outcomes. This acts as a form of emotional support and facilitates a sense of community.

Artisan entrepreneurs learn through their direct and indirect experiences that contribute to their accumulated body of knowledge. This experience is derived from observation and participation in events. The practical wisdom resulting from this experience influences their future behaviour. Learning in an entrepreneurial context refers to how to recognise and act on opportunities. This includes understanding how to start then manage a new business. Experience enables an entrepreneur to acquire knowledge about markets, resources and locations. This knowledge is helpful in starting a business as it enables valuable information about contacts, suppliers and products to be used. Entrepreneurs with prior experience have an entrepreneurial mindset that helps them evaluate opportunities. This reduces learning costs associated with assessing entrepreneurial opportunities.

Entrepreneurial experience is influenced by an individual's work history and personal characteristics. Huovinen and Tihula (2008: 154) state that entrepreneurial experience "consists of proficiency developed over the course of time (stock of experience) and knowledge accumulated through certain discrete events (stream of experience)". Entrepreneurial experience can include accumulated managerial knowledge that makes it easier to start a new business. This enables technical and practical know-how to be applied to new business ideas. Past experiences also enable existing networks and information to be used for new purposes. Entrepreneurs with past successes need to be careful to not have excess self-confidence that can lead to complacency. This means sometimes an entrepreneur may underestimate the competition and over-estimate their own capabilities.

Artisan food

There is no common definition of artisan food. The most popular way to understand artisan food is in the use of local ingredients to make handmade products. Artisan food can also be defined based on consumer perception even though in reality it may not traditionally be artisanal in nature. Artisan entrepreneurs are common in the food and beverage industry. Food artisans produce food using handmade methods typically in small batches. This means that time is spent focusing on attention to detail. Artisans normally do not use any form of machinery in the production process. Consumers are increasingly becoming interested in how food is made. This means that increased attention is placed on the ingredients and place in which the food was produced. Artisan food is made in a traditional manner often passed down through families. There is a sense of heritage in artisan food as it includes cultural elements. Artisan food is made based on traditional recipes that use few modern ingredients. This means that the food is made locally and not from imported ingredients. Provenance is an important element of artisan food as it means the place of production is known. This ensures that the ingredients and the way food is made can be traced. Food artisans are skilled craftspeople as they know how to make certain foods.

Artisans normally make a product due to personal reasons rather than financial necessity. This means that they have a sense of passion for the process of making a product and the resulting sense of enjoyment received from the final product. As a result, artisan products are perceived to have a higher quality than mass-produced products. Artisan products are made with local ingredients that are sourced based on available resources. This means that there are lower transportation costs from the making and selling of the goods. In addition, the food is generally fresher so it affects the taste. An artisan food product is normally characterised by its local ingredients and handmade nature. However, it can also be called an artisan food if it is cooked or served in a certain way. This means that there is some degree of complexity regarding how to define an artisan product. The food made by an artisan is the result of much experimentation and refinement. The process is made through traditional techniques that are known for the resulting high-quality end product.

More consumers are considering local food as a more healthier and sustainable alternative to mass-produced food. Consumers are becoming more concerned about ethical issues associated with food including where and how it was made. There are more community-minded consumers that are interested in regional economic development. This means that consumers are aware of the associated benefits of local food including employment and cultural heritage reasons. There are local and regional identities associated with food. Local food is defined based on its geographic location in terms of where it is made and produced. Thus, the distance between producer and consumer is a way to denote a local food producer. Consumers believe that locally produced food should be organically grown and additive free. This means that consumers are taking into account the natural and social environment of food production.

The artisan food sector has enjoyed significant growth due to the increased exposure on television and other media on local and handmade food. Television shows that depict the show's host travelling to meet food producers are more popular. Consumers are wanting to connect more with food in terms of how it is produced and made. In addition, community-supported farms and farmers markets have grown. Other food initiatives such as fair trade and the slow food movement have led to the increase in artisan food practices. Consumers are wanting to meet food growers to know more about their food. This sense of connection between consumer and producer can occur in person or through virtual spaces. Farmers markets enable consumers to have contact with growers and producers. They have grown at a remarkable rate and are changing the way food is bought and consumed. The direct interaction between farmer and consumer provides not only a sense of connection but also linkage to culture.

Artisan food acknowledges that there is a difference between handmade and mass-produced food. Traditional foods are often related to local culture and folklore. This means that there is specific know-how and ingredients that go into making artisan food. There is more demand for knowledge about how to make artisan food. This has led to more younger people entering the market and wanting to learn artisan techniques.

Food provides a way to communicate elements of a culture. This means that a region's identity is often characterised by the food consumed in a region. Consumers are wanting to support their local area by consuming locally grown and made food. In addition, they are more interested in sustainability, so the consumption of local food enables them to reduce environmental costs.

Artisan wine

Artisan wine comes from a small producer who usually has their own vineyards and production facilities. The wine is made using traditional winemaking processes in limited quantities. Each year the wine is different depending on the weather and soil conditions. The quality of the wine is linked to the area in which it is grown. Artisan wine makers are expected to produce wine with a consistent high quality. This means that great care is taken in bringing out the wine's characteristics in taste and texture. Artisan wine makers do not make wine for the mass-market so it can be difficult to persuade people to buy their wine. In addition, artisan wine makers have a desire to make wine in a way that links in with their social values. This means that the wine is related to their personality and personal view of life. Each artisan choses their own path in winemaking but most share a general commitment to upholding certain values.

Conclusion

This chapter has discussed the role of artisan entrepreneurship in the Indonesian food industry, thereby offering a new perspective about the way cultural heritage and innovation combine to produce new types of food. The role of art and creativity in artisan behaviour was explained in a way to understand how it impacts Indonesian culture. This enables new perspectives on artisan entrepreneurship to emerge that integrate cultural and heritage points of view. This is useful in understanding how history and context are utilised in artisan food entrepreneurship in Indonesia.

References

Chakrabarti, R. (2020). Why art matters: Artistic consumer-entrepreneurship in subsistence marketplaces. *Journal of Consumer Affairs*, 55, 134–150.

Ferreira, J. J., Fernandes, C. I., & Ratten, V. (2017). Entrepreneurship, innovation and competitiveness: What is the connection? *International Journal of Business and Globalisation*, 18(1), 73–95.

Ferreira, J. J., Ratten, V., & Dana, L. P. (2017). Knowledge spillover-based strategic entrepreneurship. *International Entrepreneurship and Management Journal*, 13(1), 161–167.

Hubner, S., Baum, M., & Frese, M. (2020). Contagion of entrepreneurial passion: Effects on employee outcomes. *Entrepreneurship Theory and Practice*, 44(6), 1112–1140.

Huovinen, J., & Tihula, S. (2008). Entrepreneurial learning in the context of portfolio entrepreneurship. *International Journal of Entrepreneurial Behaviour & Research*, 14, 152–171.

Jones, P., Klapper, R., Ratten, V., & Fayolle, A. (2018). Emerging themes in entrepreneurial behaviours, identities and contexts. *The International Journal of Entrepreneurship and Innovation*, 19(4), 233–236.

Kapoor, K., Tamilmani, K., Rana, N., Patil, P., Dwivedi, Y., & Nerur, S. (2018). Advances in social media research: Past, present and future. *Information Systems Frontier*, 20, 531–558.

Milanesi, M. (2018). Exploring passion in hobby-related entrepreneurship: Evidence from Italian cases. *Journal of Business Research*, 92, 423–430.

Phillipov, M. (2016). Using media to promote artisan food and beverages: Insights from the television industry. *British Food Journal*, 118(3), 588–602.

Rae, D., & Carswell, M. (2001). Towards a conceptual understanding of entrepreneurial learning. *Journal of Small Business and Enterprise Development*, 8(2), 150–158.

Ratten, V. (2014). Future research directions for collective entrepreneurship in developing countries: A small and medium-sized enterprise perspective. *International Journal of Entrepreneurship and Small Business*, 22(2), 266–274.

Ratten, V., & Jones, P. (2021). Entrepreneurship and management education: Exploring trends and gaps. *The International Journal of Management Education*, 19(1), 100431.

Ratten, V., & Usmanij, P. (2021). Entrepreneurship education: Time for a change in research direction? *The International Journal of Management Education*, 19(1), 100367.

Santos, G., Marques, C. S., & Ratten, V. (2019). Entrepreneurial women's networks: The case of D'Uva – Portugal Wine Girls. *International Journal of Entrepreneurial Behavior & Research*, *25*(2), 298–322.

Santos, G. M. C., Marques, C. S., Ferreira, J. J., Gerry, C., & Ratten, V. (2017). Women's entrepreneurship in Northern Portugal: Psychological factors versus contextual influences in the economic downturn. *World Review of Entrepreneurship, Management and Sustainable Development*, *13*(4), 418–440.

Suvanto, H., Niemi, J. K., & Lähdesmäki, M. (2020). Entrepreneurial identity and farmers' protein crop cultivation choices. *Journal of Rural Studies*, *75*, 174–184.

Żur, A. (2020). Entrepreneurial identity and social-business tensions – The experience of social entrepreneurs. *Journal of Social Entrepreneurship*, 1–24.

4 Knowledge management and artisan entrepreneurship in Indonesia

Vanessa Ratten

Introduction

The term 'artisan' is a debated topic as it is used in a variety of different contexts. This means that it is easy to understand what artisans do not do rather than what they do. Artisans are a form of craftmaker but are more specialised. This means that it can be hard to grasp the essence of artisanship in a definition. In this chapter, the word 'artisan' refers to a diverse array of craft practices that have been in existence for a long time. The word can be used to collectively describe craftspeople who embed a creative and cultural element to their work practices.

Knowledge is needed in order to be an artisan. Some knowledge can be easily acquired through books or interaction with others but other knowledge sources are more difficult to acquire. The term 'knowledge' refers to experiences, facts or feelings known by a person. To be classified as knowledge, an individual needs to be conscious about its value. This involves being familiar with information based on previous learning experiences. Knowledge can be used in multiple contexts and increases when it is used and shared. Artisans can benefit from the practice of knowledge management. Artisans need to be innovative in order to maintain their competitiveness. A prerequisite for innovation is the effective transfer of knowledge. Artisans can demonstrate their skills to others, but it takes actual hands-on experience to be an artisan. Therefore, novices need to acquire many different skill sets in order to become an entrepreneur. By interacting with other artisans, an individual can gain feedback and help. This enables them to learn more quickly. The attention of a skilled artisan can provide help and advice to novices. The materials required to make a product can have specific characteristics. For example, the fresh ingredients may need to be of a specific type or quality. This means that artisans develop a sense of rightness about what ingredients to use. This knowledge can take time to develop as it requires information about how a particular material can be used. This means knowing about what material to use comes from actual experience.

The structure of this chapter is as follows. Next, the importance of artisan knowledge in the creative and cultural economy is discussed. This leads to a discussion about the role of craft knowledge and the knowledge transfer process.

DOI: 10.4324/9781003187769-4

This follows with an examination of the impact of user communities and social media on artisan entrepreneurship.

Artisan knowledge

Artisans possess a practical knowledge of their craft that is the result of many years of practice. Very skilled artisans accumulate knowledge about good practices. This includes sensitive and location-specific knowledge that takes time teach to others. Some of this knowledge can also be superstitious that makes it hard to translate. Artisans also have their own knowledge based on accurate and inaccurate opinions (Ratten & Ferreira, 2017). Therefore, artisan knowledge needs to be codified in written documents to enable others to learn the craft. This is not easy to do as some artisans do not want to share their knowledge. This means that the knowledge they have is not known to others. Artisans require specific knowledge beyond that of other craftmakers.

The storing and sharing of knowledge is more easier due to the increased usage of technological tools (Apostolopoulos, Ratten, Petropoulos, Liargovas, & Anastasopoulou, 2021). Knowledge management is defined as "a management tool characterised by a set of principles along with a series of practices and techniques through which the principles are introduced, the aim of which is to create, convert, disseminate and utilise knowledge" (Palacios, Gil, & Garrigos, 2009: 292). Knowledge management involves creating, valuing and then utilising knowledge. It also implies that knowledge can be stored and distributed based on need. Therefore, it is the manipulation and control of how knowledge is shared. This means that individuals can manage knowledge in a way that creates new capabilities and increased performance (Ferreira, Fayolle, Ratten, & Raposo, 2018). Organisations need to continually acquire and utilise knowledge in order to stay competitive. For knowledge to be managed, it needs to be captured which can be a complex process. This is due to knowledge acquisition being difficult and involving a degree of subjectivity (Jones, Klapper, Ratten, & Fayolle, 2018).

Knowledge acquisition involves obtaining insights and skills. This process of knowledge generation can be derived from relationships or be a result of the collection of information. This means that knowledge acquisition is obtained from network relationships that encourage the dissemination of knowledge. To help facilitate the accumulation of knowledge, it helps to have knowledge champions. These knowledge champions can break down knowledge acquired into meaningful pieces of information (Ratten, 2020). This enables more information about the knowledge to be obtained in order to understand if it already exists or is unknown. Once knowledge is obtained it can then be shared with others. This process of knowledge sharing involves capturing the knowledge from multiple sources then ensuring it is shared to those who need it. Obtaining knowledge in a timely manner is important. This ensures individuals have the right kind of knowledge when it is needed.

In order to transmit this knowledge, it can be useful to have supervised mentorships or apprenticeships. This enables knowledge to be observed and demonstrated to others. Artisans have general knowledge about how to make products that is similar to other artisans' knowledge. They also have eclectic knowledge that is more individualised and based on personal experience. Some artisans learn their skills through professional training or educational institutions. This enables basic knowledge to be taught based on common repositories of information (Ratten, 2021a). This is an efficient way to learn about a craft and has many advantages. Practical knowledge can be taught in schools to a group of people (Ratten & Dana, 2017). This enables information about best practices to be shared. Teachers communicate knowledge in a way that can be easily understood.

Crafts knowledge includes cultivating the use of information and a commitment to the value of experience. Artisans have certain skills and abilities that they have nurtured over a period of time. This means that artisans trust their intuition and feeling about what is appropriate given the context. Artisan skill is transmitted through practical examples and modelling. The apprenticeship model is viable amongst those wanting to learn how to be an artisan due to the need to gain tacit knowledge. Knowledge can take a variety of different forms but the main way to understand knowledge is whether it takes a tacit or explicit form (Ratten, 2021b). Tacit knowledge is unwritten information that takes time to accumulate. It is hard to explain and does not exist in a written format. Explicit knowledge does take a written format and is thus easier to transfer to others. Some knowledge about artisan practices can be acquired by reading books but most is acquired through informal learning processes. This includes learning by doing in a way that transfers specific practical skills. Communicating the subtleties of a craft technique can be difficult to explain even when an artisan is shown how to do a certain technique. This means that it takes time for another person to know how to do this same technique.

Learning artisan techniques even when in direct contact with another artisan can be difficult. There is more online content including pictures and examples showing how to make a craft. This can be a useful source of information for those wanting to obtain new skills. In addition, there are videos available on how to engage in craft making activity. This includes freely available video content on websites including YouTube that are constantly being updated. Despite the various online resources available on craft practices, there is still a need to learn through direct experience. Online resources can supplement the direct experience by providing creative inspiration. This enables communities of artisans to share their practices online that facilitates discussion. In addition, online resources can help provide clarification about techniques particularly when it is hard to learn through direct experience. This facilitates a person viewing a video multiple times in order to learn at their own pace. As not everyone learns at the same pace, it can be helpful to have flexibility in replaying a video in order to learn new techniques. An example of artisan knowledge in Indonesia is the wayang kulit puppets.

Wayang kulit

Wayang kulit are leather puppets popular in Indonesia. They use the shadows thrown by puppets to tell a story. The puppets are made from elaborately detailed leather. The dalang is the puppeteer who moves the puppets around the screen. Wayang kulits have a mythical connotation in Indonesia as they symbolise good and evil. The puppets are projected onto a linen screen that has light shown on it. The stories combine educational lessons and a source of entertainment. They are an oral and intangible part of Indonesia's culture. In a play, there are several puppets used to represent different characters. During the performance, a drum is used as well as cymbol percussion instruments. Normally a wayang kulit performance begins after dark and can take a long time period. This means that some performances can go for eight to nine hours all through the night.

The play normally tells the story of the Hindu epics Ramayana and Mahabharate. The dalang uses hand movements and narration to tell the stories. The Mahabharate is an Indian epic story that tells of a family feud between the Kauravas and their cousins the Pandavas. This story has since been adapted to new contexts. In each story, the good characters are on the right and the evil characters on the left. There are deep philosophical messages portrayed in the performances. This is complemented by the gamelan orchestra and vocals used. The puppets are art works in themselves as they take a long time to make. The gamelan orchestra can consist of between 20 and 40 musicians that play a variety of instruments. In the gamelan orchestra gongs, metallophones, xylophones and strings are used. The wayang kulit was first mentioned in the 12th-century Javanese poems but is thought to be in existence before that time period. The performance is orchestrated by the puppeteer and their assistants that hand them the puppets. The stories tell the search for self-knowledge, life, love and death. Each story can combine unsolveable challenges in the form of unknown outcomes.

Craft knowledge

The knowledge needed to practice crafts can be easy or hard to obtain depending on the type of craft. Crafts that require simple repetitive action are easier to learn. However, within each craft, there can be certain skills required in order to make the craft in a fast manner. In addition, some crafts may need more skills in order to produce a high-quality product. For craft novices, actually making a product can be more difficult than they assume. This is due to an artisan's skills being embedded in their experience. Thus, the knowledge of how to make a product can be difficult to express as it is embedded in physical movements.

Craft knowledge in artisans is more than just experience as it includes physical activity. This means that it includes the manipulation and use of physical material to make a product. Thus, there is no substitute for actual hands-on experience. Online forums enable craftmakers to post pictures and make comments. As a result, a sense of community develops that enables individuals to access information regardless of geographic position. The ease of posting and accessing information online has changed the way crafts are practices. It also enables questions to be asked and answered by other artisans.

Artisans mostly exist as small enterprises that do not have the resources to generate new knowledge. This means that inter-organisational knowledge transfer is required. In order to understand how knowledge is transferred amongst artisans, social capital theory can be used. Social capital is defined as "the sum of the actual and potential resources embedded within, available through, and derived from, the network of relationships possessed by an individual or social unit" (Nahapiet & Ghoshal, 1998: 243). Knowledge is contextual so it needs to be understood based on social interactions. Despite the importance of knowledge management to the competitiveness of the cultural industries, artisans have been slow to adopt knowledge management practices. The effective management of knowledge requires four main processes: creation, storage, transfer and application (Alavi & Leidner, 2001). The creation of knowledge involves thinking about new artisan products or marketing methods. The storage refers to keeping the information in a way that can be easily accessible. Transfer involves exchanging with others useful information. Application means acting on the knowledge in a useful way.

The process of knowledge transfer

There is a well-established body of literature on knowledge transfer due to its significant role in the innovation process. Knowledge transfer in an inter-organisational context refers to the "process through which one organisation learns from the experience and knowledge of another for gaining or sustaining a competitive advantage" (Martinkenaite, 2011: 54). Knowledge transfer between artisans eases the way new ideas are introduced into the market. Artisan engagement refers to high relational involvement in situations where multiple artisans work together on joint projects. Knowledge transfer involves exchanging knowledge that is useful from one context to another. The capability of artisans to absorb new knowledge depends on their knowledge base. This means that the capacity to recognise and apply new knowledge can vary amongst artisans. The interpretation of knowledge can be made difficult when artisans have different opinions and beliefs about its usefulness.

Knowledge helps artisans maintain a strategic competitive advantage in the marketplace. Therefore, knowledge can be developed through a range of processes including experience and improvisation. In order to strengthen the artisan, industry knowledge needs to be shared. Knowledge transfer is a process of information exchange. This is a complex task as it requires the accurate interpretation of information. De Luca and Rubio (2019) suggest that people learn on two levels: a lower level and higher level. The lower level refers to repetition of past behaviours that are improved over time. This involves focusing on routine activities that are conducted in the short term. Higher level learning involves the development of new insights that change existing assumptions. This enables new knowledge to be created.

The possession of knowledge can help guide an artisan towards success. It provides an artisan with useful information that enhances their entrepreneurial capability. Knowledge transfer involves a reciprocal relationship between the giver and receiver. Latilla, Frattini, Petruzzelli and Berner (2019: 1336) suggest that craft organisations are involved in "the production of high symbolic value artifacts, resulted of largely manual (handmade) processes obtained through the work of high-skilled craftsmen". Thus, artisan knowledge mainly exists in the minds of the artisans as a result of their working experience. This means that it is not expressed in an explicit way but rather is manifested in a tacit way. Therefore, this form of knowledge requires actual demonstrations. Artisans have a form of cultural intelligence. They confer a sense of exclusivity to products they make. This unique position means they have an aura that is difficult to copy. Artisan knowledge is the result of abilities and talent used to make products. An artisan who effectively manages their knowledge can build a good reputation.

Knowledge transfer involves articulating information to others in a way that is mutually understood. To do this, it involves the modification of existing knowledge to a new context. Knowledge is transferred when one person purposefully receives and uses the knowledge from other individuals. In the context of artisans, it can be useful to focus on how other artisans transfer knowledge through tools and tasks. Tools refer to equipment and technology needed to make artisan products. Tasks involve the actual actions required by an artisan to make a product.

Learning occurs when knowledge is used to solve problems. Knowledge is an elusive concept that can be best described as useful information that is accumulated over time. This means what an artisan knows and how they use this knowledge is important. In order for knowledge to be useful, it needs to be harnessed and leveraged in the right way. This involves transferring information in a way that makes sense to others. One way to transfer information is by selecting key themes that can be shared with others. For knowledge to be transferred individuals need to be willing to share information. This means collaborating with others through cooperative relationships.

Knowledge and expertise are part of the success of artisan entrepreneurs. The most successful practices are taught to up-and-coming artisans to ensure the craft remains in existence. There are many different forms of knowledge existing amongst artisans. This includes knowledge of things that can be used in the production process. This might include information about certain objects that can help an artisan make a product. There is also knowledge of how to do things that is learned over time. This may include the steps required and the associated resources required to make this happen. The making of an artisan product can be done in different ways so consideration of the individual skills and context is required. In order for others to learn this practice, it can be helpful for an artisan to show how they are making a product and the necessary steps required. This might include the know-how in terms of the capability to undertake a task or the know-why in terms of the reasons for the actions. Managing knowledge is a prerequisite for higher levels of productivity.

Utilisation of social networks

Social networks are important for entrepreneurial success as they enable individuals to accumulate knowledge. The ability to develop and maintain a personal network is a key skill needed by artisan entrepreneurs. Social networks give access to resources that entrepreneurs need to build their business. Individuals as members of a social network are dependent on the exchange of resources. Entrepreneurs try to reduce uncertainty by being members of a social network. Therefore, artisan entrepreneurship is dependent on access to different kinds of resources.

Social networks are part of asset parsimony as they enable quick access to necessary resources. Asset parsimony is defined as "the effort needed to acquire the minimum assets at the lowest possible cost, in order to pursue the company's goals" (Jenssen, 2001: 104). This gives entrepreneurs some degree of flexibility in how they manage their business practices. A social network provides a way for an entrepreneur to take advantage of resources when the need arises. This flexibility is helpful when the pace of business growth is unknown, and there is a degree of fluctuation in market demand. Access to resources can save an entrepreneur time and money. Entrepreneurs without a social network may have a difficult time in creating networks. This means that entrepreneurs constantly use their existing networks as a source of information. They also develop their initial network into a larger network over time. The individuals in the initial network can introduce other people to the network or give advice about who else to contact. The more contacts an entrepreneur has increases the probability that a specific resource or type of information can be accessed. However, the quality of network contacts can be more important than the quantity of social contacts. In a social network, the bonds between members can be described as strong or weak. Strong ties imply a close bond between network members. This enables higher levels of trust to exist between members because of the high level of interaction. Weak ties refer to network members with infrequent contact.

Artisan entrepreneurs often engage in social entrepreneurship due to the hybrid nature of their businesses combing both profit and non-profit objectives. Social entrepreneurship occurs when an entrepreneur has a dual mission of both financial outcomes and social impact. Social entrepreneurship plays an important role in the adoption of business strategies that contribute to economic development and social change. Increasingly social entrepreneurship is being adopted by artisan entrepreneurs due to initiatives by stakeholders in pursuing joint cultural and social goals.

There is a consensus in the literature that the defining characteristics of a social entrepreneur is the ability to combine social value with business strategy. Social enterprises utilise a wide range of business models to achieve their social objectives. Due to the hybrid nature of social enterprises, they can ensure the cooperation of different stakeholders including local communities, government, artisans and private sector organisations. This enables social forms of innovation to occur through stakeholder relationships.

Social innovation involves adopting creative practices with the purpose of solving social problems. Social innovations can refer to new products, organisational forms and processes. This means that there are many ways innovations can be considered as having a social component. Social innovators mobilise resources in order to transform society. They do this by engaging with beneficiaries of the change in order to increase access to resources. The key aim of social innovation is to empower people by supporting relational and structural change.

Artisan social entrepreneurship is a process that uses artisanry to create innovative solutions to social problems. This can be done by harnessing the capacities and ideas from an artisan context. Social entrepreneurship marks an ethical shift in the way entrepreneurship is conducted. This means incorporating social benefits as the central mission of an artisan business, thereby extending the benefits of artisan entrepreneurship to a social context. This means thinking differently about the value created from an artisan by investing in social goals.

Social media and intellectual capital

Social media is recognised by artisans as a way of facilitating communication with others about their products. It enhances public relations and expands their customer base. Digital technologies have enabled artisans to reduce their communication costs and enabled the transmission of new types of information. Digital technologies such as social media have led to new approaches for knowledge creation and coordination to be adopted. This has enhanced the way knowledge is stored and shared. Digital applications such as annotation in online discussions can provide useful feedback and comments.

Artisan entrepreneurs have a high level of intellectual capital that differentiates them from other entrepreneurs. Marr and Moustaghfir (2005: 1116) define intellectual capital as "any valuable intangible resource gained through experience and learning that can be used in the production of further wealth". Artisan entrepreneurs have intellectual capital in the form of attitudes, knowledge and skills. Intellectual capital includes the invisible assets of an entrepreneur such as managerial skills and technological knowledge. These skills are important resources for the long-term success. Klein and Prusak (1994) suggest that intellectual capital includes any form of intellectual material that can be leveraged to create a higher-value asset. This means that it is the result of information-based assets including competencies and skills. Moreover, intangible property rights such as brand name and reputation contribute to an individual's intellectual capital. This enables them to utilise customer relationships in a strategic way. Intellectual capital is difficult to imitate because of its individual-specific nature.

Artisans need to utilise their intellectual capital through a process of dynamic capabilities in order to compete in the global marketplace. Teece, Pisano and Shuen (1997: 516) defined dynamic capabilities as "a firm's ability to integrate, build and reconfigure internal and external competences to address rapidly changing environments". This means purposefully extending their resource base in order to capitalise on new opportunities. The way artisans create or modify their existing products is a result of market demands. Eisenhardt and Martin (2000) suggest that markets are constantly changing in terms of colliding, splitting, evolving and dying. This means that artisan firms need to consider how they can reconfigure their products to fit emerging market needs.

Teece (2007) suggested that firms can utilise their dynamic capabilities by sensing, seizing and transforming their strategy. Sensing involves predicting threats and opportunities before they occur in the market. This involves understanding the changes in the environment. Seizing involves acting on opportunities as they emerge in the marketplace. This is important in leveraging capabilities and entering new markets. Transforming involves changing the firm's strategy to suit new market needs.

Artisans utilise their knowledge and experience to create products so domain-specific knowledge is highly relevant to their production techniques. Nordqvist and Frishammar (2019: 79) define domain-specific knowledge as "knowledge about something that is gained by means of experiments, study and experience within the specific technical domain in which the work is performed". It enables an artisan to produce products at a specific quality and output level. Procedural knowledge refers to steps needed to perform a task. This is a distinct type of knowledge as it influences how artisans undertake work and engage in collaboration. Artisans gain procedural knowledge from previous experience in designing products. It resides in the minds of artisans as it involves knowledge about how to market a product. In order for individuals to learn artisan skills, they must take a conscious step to tap into the knowledge of existing artisans.

A big part of the development process in innovation derives from the input and feedback of users. The role of users in innovation tends to be underestimated but increasingly they are being utilised as a way to advance the innovation development process. Community of users are using online and social media platforms to discuss innovation. This provides a good mechanism to disseminate ideas and obtain advice about new developments. Users are motivated to be innovative in order to gain advantages in terms of usage consumption patterns. In addition, there are non-profit motives such as willingness to be a member of a community that further influences the innovation process. The cost of innovation depends on the type of resources required. Users can create low cost and quick innovations based on their knowledge.

The performance of a locality is impacted by the complexity of actors that interact for business purposes. This means that each locality needs to be considered as a unique place that has its own sense of identity. The success of an artisan business is more dependent on the exercise of specialist knowledge than on market forces. Artisan knowledge is dependent on manual skills and cognitive abilities. Artisans have certain know-how that is embodied with their craft. This means that artisan products depend on intimate knowledge of a craft. An artisan's tacit understandings of a craft are more important than their general knowledge. Artisans simultaneously construct products based on their interaction with them.

Artisan knowledge in a community context

Artisan entrepreneurs are powerful contributors to local communities and act as catalysts of change. Community-based entrepreneurs are established and governed to promote benefits to a community. They are similar to social enterprises due to the non-profit nature of many of their business activities. They have a collectivist structure that focuses on a group of people, rather than just individual needs. The success of a community enterprise is the result of how specific cultural values have been embedded in business practices. Naturally, academics, practitioners and policymakers are paying increased attention to artisan entrepreneurs because of their role in cultural development. Artisan entrepreneurship is a popular topic due to the growing fascination with culture, history and the handicraft industry. The entrepreneurship literature tends to glorify individual entrepreneurs who create value through technological innovation whilst diminishing the role cultural entrepreneurs plays in society.

The link between artisans and entrepreneurs represents a new frontier in entrepreneurship research. This link builds on the existing literature in the anthropology, sociology, tourism and community development fields. Social scientists have for a long time researched the way culture is practised in society through creative pursuits. In fact, the sense of culture is evident in most forms of artisan entrepreneurship. Lumpkin, Bacq and Pidduck (2018) suggest that community level activities can be understood through sociological, economic, anthropology and political science. Entrepreneurship is touted as a way to incorporate cultural elements within business practices. There has been a tendency to focus on high-tech products within entrepreneurship practices, but this has changed with more focus being placed on preserving an area's cultural heritage. As a result, there are now more efforts to spur entrepreneurship based on cultural practices. Artisan entrepreneurship has played a key role in the revitalisation of communities by aligning business practices to cultural heritage. This is due to artisan entrepreneurship involving the creation, development and management of artisan businesses. A defining feature of artisan entrepreneurship is in the way cultural elements are incorporated into products. This enables entrepreneurs to respect the past whilst embracing the future. A related feature of artisan entrepreneurship is in the way artisans reconcile cultural values with modern practices. This can be a challenge due to alternating socio-cultural needs.

Artisan entrepreneurs belong to diverse realities due to their geographic position and history. Therefore, artisan entrepreneurship can be considered in terms of urban, rural and remote practices. Urban practices refer to the use of culture within city-based artisans. There has been more emphasis on handicrafts amongst community groups in cities. Rural practices involve farm-based artisan activity that occurs in a country environment. This occurs when specific use of land or material is required for the artisan business. Remote practices refer to artisans who operate in areas that are geographically difficult to enter. Due to the remoteness of the area, it may mean that the artisans are involved in unique practices that only occur in that location.

Conclusion

Artisans have distinct forms of knowledge that differentiate them from other types of craftmakers. Due to the way culture is embedded within artisanship, it is important that knowledge is transferred to others. To do this takes some time as knowledge can be both tacit and explicit. This chapter examined the different types and ways that knowledge can be exchanged based on artisan practices, thereby highlighting the need for artisans to implement knowledge management practices.

References

Alavi, M., & Leidner, D. E. (2001). Knowledge management and knowledge management systems: Conceptual foundations and research issues. *MIS Quarterly*, 107–136.

Apostolopoulos, N., Ratten, V., Petropoulos, D., Liargovas, P., & Anastasopoulou, E. (2021). Agri-food sector and entrepreneurship during the Covid-19 crisis: A systematic literature review and research agenda. *Strategic Change*, 30(2), 159–167.

De Luca, P., & Cano Rubio, M. (2019). The curve of knowledge transfer: A theoretical model. *Business Process Management Journal*, 25(1), 10–26.

Eisenhardt, K. M., & Martin, J. A. (2000). Dynamic capabilities: What are they? *Strategic Management Journal*, 21(10–11), 1105–1121.

Ferreira, J. J., Fayolle, A., Ratten, V., & Raposo, M. (Eds.). (2018). *Entrepreneurial universities*. Cheltenham: Edward Elgar Publishing.

Jenssen, J. I. (2001). Social networks, resources and entrepreneurship. *The International Journal of Entrepreneurship and Innovation*, 2(2), 103–109.

Jones, P., Klapper, R., Ratten, V., & Fayolle, A. (2018). Emerging themes in entrepreneurial behaviours, identities and contexts. *The International Journal of Entrepreneurship and Innovation*, 19(4), 233–236.

Klein, D. A., & Prusak, L. (1994). *Characterising intellectual capital*. Cambridge, MA: Centre for Business Innovation, Ernst and Young.

Latilla, V. M., Frattini, F., Petruzzelli, A. M., & Berner, M. (2019). Knowledge management and knowledge transfer in arts and crafts organizations: Evidence from an exploratory multiple case-study analysis. *Journal of Knowledge Management*, 23(7), 1335–1354.

Lumpkin, G. T., Bacq, S., & Pidduck, R. J. (2018). Where change happens: Community-level phenomena in social entrepreneurship research. *Journal of Small Business Management*, 56(1), 24–50.

Marr, B., & Moustaghfir, K. (2005). Defining intellectual capital: A three-dimensional approach. *Management Decision*, 43, 1114–1128.

Martinkenaite, I. (2011). Antecedents and consequences of interorganizational knowledge transfer: Emerging themes and openings for further research. *Baltic Journal of Management*, 6(1), 53–70.

Nahapiet, J., & Ghoshal, S. (1998). Social capital, intellectual capital, and the organizational advantage. *Academy of Management Review*, 23(2), 242–266.

Nordqvist, S., & Frishammar, J. (2019). Knowledge types to progress the development of sustainable technologies: A case study of Swedish demonstration plants. *International Entrepreneurship and Management Journal*, 15(1), 75–95.

Palacios, D., Gil, I., & Garrigos, F. (2009). The impact of knowledge management on innovation and entrepreneurship in the biotechnology and telecommunications industries. *Small Business Economics*, *32*(3), 291–301.

Ratten, V. (2020). Coronavirus and international business: An entrepreneurial ecosystem perspective. *Thunderbird International Business Review*, *62*(5), 629–634.

Ratten, V. (2021a). Sport entrepreneurial ecosystems and knowledge spillovers. *Knowledge Management Research & Practice*, *19*(1), 43–52.

Ratten, V. (2021b). Covid-19 and entrepreneurship: Future research directions. *Strategic Change*, *30*(2), 91–98.

Ratten, V., & Dana, L. P. (2017). Sustainable entrepreneurship, family farms and the dairy industry. *International Journal of Social Ecology and Sustainable Development*, *8*(3), 114–129.

Ratten, V., & Ferreira, J. J. (2017). Future research directions for cultural entrepreneurship and regional development. *International Journal of Entrepreneurship and Innovation Management*, *21*(3), 163–169.

Teece, D. J. (2007). Explicating dynamic capabilities: The nature and microfoundations of (sustainable) enterprise performance. *Strategic Management Journal*, *28*(13), 1319–1350.

Teece, D. J., Pisano, G., & Shuen, A. (1997). Dynamic capabilities and strategic management. *Strategic Management Journal*, *18*(7), 509–533.

5 Indonesian migrant entrepreneurs

A comparison of two cohorts in Malaysia

Hamizah Abd Hamid

Introduction

Research focusing on migration, in particular, within the scope of migrant entrepreneurs has largely focused on Western-based countries, leaving a gap in understanding intra-regional migration, especially towards non-Western migrant-receiving countries (Aliaga-Isla & Rialp, 2013). Additionally, research within this area has not fully captured the interest among academics in developing countries (Mosbah, Debili, & Merazga, 2018), which can be explained by societal diversity and lack of public information on migration in such nations (developing, non-Western) (Abd Hamid, O'Kane, & Everett, 2019), attributing to the complexity in fleshing out the phenomenon. To this end, this chapter navigates these uncharted waters by focusing on the historical contexts of intra-regional migration through the perspectives of ethnic migrant entrepreneurs.

In addition to the traditional migration from non-Western countries to Western countries, the global migration landscape is observing migration from non-Western countries within their regions. These changes in migration pattern imply a change in the type of migrants these countries are attracting, which include skilled and educated individuals, as opposed to the traditional low-skilled workers. Such knowledge about the mechanisms and experiences of migration in such countries, especially in Asia, is rather limited in the literature (Abel, Raymer, & Guan, 2019; Hugo, 2005).

A shifting trend in global mobility calls for a deeper understanding of migration to such countries. In this regard, this chapter responds to this gap by exploring the experiences of Indonesian migrant entrepreneurs (IMEs) in Malaysia. This chapter focuses on the historical dimension in migration, informed by the experiences of two migrant cohorts. Doing so enables us to elucidate the contextual factors surrounding entrepreneurship activities within the scope of migration. Migrant entrepreneurs as a context provide us with accounts of actors, networks and institutions involved in the migrant-sending and migrant-receiving countries (Barrett & Vershinina, 2017; Kloosterman & Rath, 2001). Further, unlike expatriates, migrant entrepreneurs are considered as individuals more closely linked with in-group networks, given the published challenges experienced in the migrant-receiving country. In this aspect, this chapter provides a

DOI: 10.4324/9781003187769-5

contextual account of Indonesian entrepreneurship through the perspective of migrant entrepreneurs.

This chapter's setting, Malaysia, represents a country with comparatively low resources (when compared with traditional migrant-receiving countries) in dealing with foreigners, while Indonesia is selected as a migrant-sending country to be investigated given their propensities as one of the largest diaspora community globally (World Bank, 2017). Although emigration from Indonesia to Malaysia has been consistently high, a wave of migration from Indonesia is observed in 1997 to 1998 influenced by political reform and financial crisis which encourages the migration of skilled and economically prosperous individuals (Arifin, Ananta, Wilujeng Wahyu Utami, Budi Handayani, & Pramono, 2015). Such phenomenon exacerbates the embeddedness of entrepreneurs into their socio-cultural context, as documented in Indonesian entrepreneurs (Anggadwita, Luturlean Bachruddin, Ramadani, & Ratten, 2017).

The structure of the chapter is as per following. First, this chapter discusses the theoretical framework, then followed by a clarification of the context chosen in this chapter (Indonesian migration to Malaysia across two time frames). Next, the methods and the findings of this chapter are explained, followed by a discussion of the findings and concluded with a summary of the research and recommendations for future studies.

Literature review

The embeddedness framework

This chapter is outlined by the embeddedness framework (Jack & Anderson, 2002; Kloosterman, 2010; Kloosterman & Rath, 2001; Uzzi, 1997) to understand IMEs' embeddedness within their home and host countries with regards to migration and entrepreneurship activities. Embeddedness is referred to as the complexity and extent of individuals to an environment (Jack & Anderson, 2002; Uzzi, 1997), influenced by history and linkages among members (Marsden, 1981). As entrepreneurship is a result of the dynamics of the entrepreneur and the local context through the embeddedness process (Jack & Anderson, 2002; Ozdemir, Moran, Zhong, & Bliemel, 2016), this framework has been applied in studies in exploring the way entrepreneurs perceive and exploit opportunities within a specific setting. This includes female entrepreneurs (Essers, Benschop, & Doorewaard, 2010), entrepreneurs in depleted communities (McKeever, Jack, & Anderson, 2015) and post-war Soviet entrepreneurs (Rodgers, Vershinina, Williams, & Theodorakopoulos, 2019).

These studies demonstrate the way entrepreneurship activities are contextually bound; however, to our best knowledge, a time-based comparison on entrepreneurship activities particularly in ethnic migrant entrepreneurship has yet to be done. Adding historical accounts could enrich our knowledge on the selected entrepreneurial phenomenon, especially in contextually sensitive topics such as ethnic migrant entrepreneurship (Koning & Verver, 2013; Peters, 2002).

Through exploring the migration and entrepreneurial experiences of migrants from different cohorts, this chapter is able to gauge how such communities navigate the social and institutional environments of the host country, based on their motivations and mechanisms of migration. As examples, research on Chinese migrant entrepreneurs in Thailand by Koning and Verver (2013) illustrated the differences in the way in which two generations of Chinese migrants in business perceive their identities in the host country, whereas Storti's (2014) study of Italian migrants in Germany shows the way post-war migrants deal with the host country through small entrepreneurship ventures. As such entrepreneurs are highly embedded within their contexts for resources and entrepreneurial opportunities, this chapter further examines embeddedness in entrepreneurial activities using a time-based comparison.

Embeddedness in ethnic migrant entrepreneurship

The embeddedness framework in this chapter is outlined by the mixed embeddedness model, which is a model specifically designed to study ethnic migrant entrepreneurs. According to the mixed embeddedness model, ethnic migrant entrepreneurs are embedded within their particular opportunity structure, influenced by layers of societal factors within the host–home country dynamics (Jones, Ram, Edwards, Kiselinchev, & Muchenje, 2014; Kloosterman, 2010; Kloosterman & Rath, 2001). In particular, ethnic migrant entrepreneurs are embedded in the internal, micro-environment of their entrepreneurial ventures and the external structure of the host country through complex community-level and nation-level environments (Abd Hamid, Everett, & O'Kane, 2018; Ram, Theodorakopoulos, & Jones, 2008). More importantly, this model specifies the role of political, spatial, economic and regulatory contexts affecting an ethnic migrant entrepreneur's entrepreneurial venture (Carter, Mwaura, Ram, Trehan, & Jones, 2015; Jones et al., 2014; Kloosterman, 2010). As such, for this chapter, IMEs are conceptualised as embedded within the dynamics of their home countries and the host country, which will hold important implications for the process of starting a venture in the host country as a migrant.

Intra-regional migration, diaspora waves and embeddedness

Embeddedness within the scope of ethnic migrant entrepreneurship is operationalised as entrepreneurs' home country relations within the setting of the host country, which covers layers of societal and contextual factors within the host–home country dynamics. Through the embeddedness lens, this chapter investigates the differences and similarities of the ways pre-1997 and post-1997 IMEs deal with intra-regional migration and entrepreneurship activities. IMEs from different waves of intra-regional migration are embedded within the history, structures and processes experienced in their home and host countries. Consider these two situations: (1) a migrant from a politically unstable nation fleeing his/her country pushed into entrepreneurship due to lack of employment opportunities and (2) a migrant from a relatively stable country equipped with resources for entrepreneurship being self-employed in a host country. Ethnic migrant entrepreneurs from Situation (2) are likely to fare more fortunately than entrepreneurs from the first situation, as they are more equipped to start a new venture in a foreign nation. In this regard, the way an ethnic migrant entrepreneur deals with the process of migration and entrepreneurial venture commencement in the host country is almost contingent with his/her resources and relations to his/her home country.

To understand the differences between entrepreneurs in Situation (1) and Situation (2), this chapter utilises a time-based boundary to complement the embeddedness framework outlining this chapter. A time-based boundary will delineate individuals' experiences with regards to time and environment (Ancona, Okhuysen, & Perlow, 2001; Kim, Bansal, & Haugh, 2019) given the socially constructed nature of time (Bluedorn & Standifer, 2006). As this chapter is examining variances in experiences, different points of time are taken into account (Bluedorn & Standifer, 2006), especially for experiences with regards to migration, as time-sensitive large-scale changes (e.g. the Arab spring or Brexit) may impact migrants' resources and opportunities (Erel & Ryan, 2019).

Research focus

The embeddedness framework has been applied to many community-based entrepreneurship topics (e.g. see McKeever et al. (2015)). Although these studies have assisted our understanding about the way entrepreneurship activities are bounded contextually, a time-based comparison on entrepreneurship activities has yet to be done, especially within ethnic migrant entrepreneurship context. In this regard, this chapter's research focus is *How do ethnic migrant entrepreneurs from different waves of migration build their ventures in the host country?* To adhere to the embeddedness framework, this chapter focuses on the migration of IMEs to Malaysia, comparing two groups of IMEs (pre-1997 and post-1997 IMEs). Here, particular attention is paid to both groups' home country embeddedness in the host country in their process of migration and building a venture.

Indonesian migration to Malaysia: context and focus

Intra-regional migrations especially in Asia are largely influenced by relationships maintained by migrants in the migrant-receiving and migrant-sending countries (Hugo, 2014), which shape their embeddedness within the region. Migration to Malaysia has seen a positive increase since the 1980s (United Nations, 2019), in which most of the migrants come to Malaysia to fill the demand for low-skilled jobs (Kaur, 2008). Malaysia is particularly attractive as a labour market to migrants from neighbouring countries such as Indonesia, the Philippines, China, Bangladesh, India, Thailand, Myanmar and Pakistan, given its stable economic growth that induces job creation (World Bank, 2019). Migration to Malaysia is further encouraged by Malaysia's geographic location, which is centrally located in Southeast Asia's most congested migration route; this facilitates the relocation of many multinational companies to the nation which encourages a large demand for foreign workers (Bastide, in press). With regards to the demographics of migrants received by Malaysia, as of the year 2019, the largest migrant-sending countries are Indonesia, followed by the Philippines, Bangladesh, Thailand, Myanmar, Nepal, India and China (United Nations, 2019), with consistent increase in migration from Indonesia, as shown in Figure 5.1.

Indonesia as a migrant-sending nation, however, is a country characterised by its multi-ethnic and multi-cultural society encompassing over 200 ethnic groups. Its national culture is largely influenced by various religions including Islam, Christianity, Buddhism and Hinduism. Indonesia diaspora are primarily prominent in Malaysia, Saudi Arabia and the United Arab Emirates, mainly employed in service and manufacturing sectors (United Nations, 2019; World Bank, 2017). Present-day Malaysia and Indonesia share a similar history, given that both countries belong in the Indo–Malay archipelago and are connected through trade, migration and marriage (Liow, 2005a). Indonesian migrants' permanent presence in major Malaysian urban areas is facilitated by Indonesians who were able to obtain Malaysian permanent resident status (Wong, 2006). The Islam-related affinity, racial and linguistic similarities shared common history and geographical proximity in the Malay Archipelago have largely defined Malaysia–Indonesia bilateral relations. These commonalities and similarities have been assumed under the underlying concept of *serumpun* (Khalid & Yacob, 2012), described as the organising principle of Malaysia–Indonesia relations (Liow, 2005a, 2005b). Therefore, within the framework of embeddedness, Indonesian migrants are

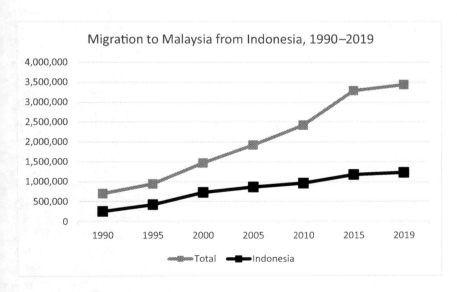

Figure 5.1 Migration from Indonesia to Malaysia

largely embedded by their home country in Malaysia. This concept can be seen in the propensity for Indonesian migrants to live in clusters of Indonesian societies in the host country even though they are able to converse and communicate with the locals in Malaysia.

In general, Malaysia has made more economic development progress than Indonesia; therefore, for Indonesians, migrating to Malaysia is seen as a chance to improve their lives. In the early 20th century, large-scale migration from Indonesia to Malaysia started to develop when the British colonial government decided to recruit Java Island Indonesian workers from the then-Dutch East Indies. This was based on the rationale of Javanese and Malays sharing similar cultures and religions, thus leading to the assumptions that they might assimilate easily (Kaur, 2004). Closeness in culture in the context of Indonesians in Malaysia enables intercultural communication through the similarities in language (Abd Hamid et al., 2018; Jamaludin, Senik, Abd Hamid, & Muhamad, 2020). In relation to the locals' favourability towards certain migrant groups (Weiss & Tulin, in press), such closeness in culture provides Indonesian migrants in Malaysia leverage against migrants from other countries (e.g. migrants from Bangladesh and the Philippines) especially in communicating with the locals. Cultural closeness is complemented by geographical proximity; there are six migration corridors from Indonesia to Malaysia spanning air, water and land travel, which further encourages the dynamic mobility of individuals from Indonesia to Malaysia (and vice versa) (Spaan & van Naerssen, 2018).

The high number of Indonesian migrants to Malaysia is partly a result of the rapid transformation of Malaysia during the 1980s and 1990s, in which most of them arriving for employment. Aptly called Indonesian labour force, *Tenaga Kerja Indonesia* or TKI, Indonesian workers have been documented to be willing to work long hours for low wages. Indonesian men are generally employed in the construction sector, whereas Indonesian women generally can be found working as domestic help, factory employees and restaurant workers (Khalid & Yacob, 2012; Rahman & Fee, 2009).

An important event in the history of Indonesia is during the economic downturn in 1997. The devaluation of Thai Baht; the economic crisis led to a political one, called *Orde Baru*, which is a political restructuring that impacts, among others, the private sector in Indonesia which entails the closing of many businesses and industries causing business and employment loss (Munandar, 2003). A wave of emigration around 1997 to 1998 ensues, partly as a result of such political reform and financial crisis (Arifin et al., 2015); this mainly shapes Indonesia's emigration landscape in which more high-skilled emigration is witnessed during such times. This partly explains Indonesian migration motivations to other countries during the late 1990s, especially to Malaysia, composed by resource-rich professionals and business owners (Hasanah, 2015). Indeed, Indonesian migration to Malaysia, pre- and post-late-1990s has shaped a multifaceted horizon of migrants, from unskilled workers to skilled professionals. With regard to this, a qualitative study is undertaken on IMEs who came to Malaysia before 1997 post 1997 to further understand the dynamics of embeddedness in ethnic migrant entrepreneurship, focusing on the context of Indonesia–Malaysia.

Research methods

This chapter employs a qualitative design in enabling the investigation of the phenomenon in its real-life context (Yin, 2014) and builds detailed narratives displaying the process (Flyvbjerg, 2006). In this chapter, purposive sampling is applied in selecting the participants of this chapter to facilitate comparisons (Miles & Huberman, 1994), which is instrumental in the initial stages of data collection planning (Denzin & Lincoln, 2011). The sampling of Indonesian entrepreneurs and their ventures was guided by the following criteria:

- Indonesian entrepreneurs who arrive in Malaysia since before 1997 and after 1997
- Indonesian entrepreneurs who have experienced operating at least one business venture in Malaysia
- Indonesian entrepreneurs whose ventures have been operating for one or more financial years in Malaysia

For consistency reasons, this chapter focuses on IMEs in greater Kuala Lumpur, Malaysia. To achieve a nuanced perspective of the phenomenon, interviews were held with three key societal association informants, namely an Indonesian embassy representative focusing on trade and migration, a community leader and the president of an Indonesian trade association in the migrant-receiving country. Such perspectives encourage understanding development-related migration topics (De Haas, 2010; Gamlen, Cummings, & Vaaler, 2019). The details of the informants in this chapter are summarised in Tables 5.1 and 5.2.

Table 5.1 Sources of primary data for the study

Name	Year of arrival	Gender	Education	Form of business	Details of entrepreneurial venture
IME1	Pre-1997	Male	Master's degree	General partnership	*Jamu* (Indonesian herb products)
IME2	Pre-1997	Male	Upper secondary	General partnership	Logistics
IME3	Post-1997	Male	Master's degree	General partnership	Indonesian FMCGs (fast-moving consumer goods)
IME4	Post-1997	Female	Bachelor's degree	General partnership	Spa services and products
IME5	Post-1997	Female	Master's degree	General partnership	Indonesian FMCGs

(*Continued*)

Table 5.1 (Continued)

Name	Year of arrival	Gender	Education	Form of business	Details of entrepreneurial venture
IME6	Pre-1997	Male	Upper secondary	General partnership	Logistics
IME7	Post-1997	Male	Bachelor's degree	General partnership	Teakwood furniture
IME8	Post-1997	Female	Bachelor's degree	General partnership	Indonesian-based food
IME9	Pre-1997	Male	Upper secondary	Sole trader	Textile and groceries
IME10	Pre-1997	Male	Diploma	General partnership	Indonesian FMCGs

Table 5.2 Summary of supplementary respondents

Respondent type	Name (coded)	Details
Embassy representative specialising on trade	ITE	Embassy representative focusing on migration and trade
Within-community trade association leader	ITL	Leader of an Indonesian trade association in Malaysia, members of the association conduct and operate small to medium-sized entrepreneurial ventures in Malaysia
Within-community association leader	ICL	Leader of a community association of Indonesian migrants in Malaysia. This association focuses on the well-being of Indonesian compatriots in the migrant-receiving country

Secondary data sources were used for cross-checking purposes, through validating the findings from the interviews and gathering further information from partial sources. This was conducted during and after data collection in three stages: first, employing a case-level review of community-centric entrepreneurial activities referred from community documents and sources; the second step involved conducting a firm-level examination underlined by the information from company-based sources including websites and company documents; and the third consisting of an individual-level assessment of the entrepreneurs was conducted based on the information available on their company websites.

The participants were contacted via phone prior to interviewing and were given details about this chapter. Interviews within the duration of 25 to 90 were digitally recorded, with the consent of the interviewees. In total, 735 minutes of face-to-face interviews were conducted (thirteen sessions). All interviews were held at the participants' business/formal premises to have a deeper understanding of their responses. The body of data was divided into two categories: IMEs who have arrived in Malaysia before the year 1997 (pre-1997 IMEs), and IMEs who have arrived in Malaysia after 1997 (post-1997 IMEs) to understand the way IMEs differ in terms of their migration and entrepreneurial motivations. An abductive approach was undertaken to analyse the data, in which a deductive approach was employed using the embeddedness framework. An inductive approach followed, whereby the observed narratives were analysed by identifying themes and patterns. The themes were then synthesised in accordance with the embeddedness framework.

Results

Five of the interviewees came to Malaysia in 1998 (the respondents mentioned that the financial crisis in Indonesia which was at its peak in 1998 is one of the main reasons they left the country), while the years of entry for the rest of the IME interviewees are between 1969 and 1990. Comparisons are made based on the multi-focal date of arrival for the studied IMEs especially with regards to the contextual aspects underlying their migration motivations and mechanisms. The interviewees have at a minimum upper secondary education qualification and have different personal and professional motivations to migrate to Malaysia. Only one of the businesses is in the form of sole proprietorship, whereas the rest are in the form of general partnerships. It can be observed that all of the companies studied in this chapter have at least one home country element in their operations, shown in the characteristics of the products or services that they offer and/or their initial target market.

Motivations of migration to Malaysia: push factors from the migrant-sending country, pull factors from the migrant-receiving country

To contextualise the factors encouraging the IMEs' migration to Malaysia, the motivations to emigrate are categorised into two main dimensions: push and pull factors. Push factors in this aspect include the political contexts of the migrant-sending country and employment reasons to migrate. Pull factors refer to the aspects of the host country that attract IMEs to migrate, which include the prospects for business opportunities and family reunification.

Only one pre-1997 IME came to Malaysia due to push factors from their home country. IME10, an herbal trader (or *jamu*, in Bahasa Indonesia), explained that he came to Malaysia for employment reasons and decided to build his own venture in the host country:

> *I moved to Malaysia in 1980, as an employee with a trading company that specialises in Indonesian herbal products, or jamu and cosmetics.*
>
> (IME10)

For the post-1997 IMEs, the respondents commented that the political changes happening around the late 1990s were primarily a reason for them to emigrate. Further investigation into this reason revealed that the political changes had potential detrimental effects towards their well-being in their home country, which primarily influencing their employment and entrepreneurial activities. This is illustrated by the following comments from the community leader (ICL), embassy representative (ITE) and an entrepreneur in the teakwood industry, IME7:

> *Indonesian entrepreneurs come to Malaysia with different background and stories, depending on the year of arrival.*
>
> (ICL)

> *Those that I mentioned who came later, these are the people who left Indonesia due to the political changes that was happening during the time, I were experiencing some political changes in the government, which is the end of Orde Baru, resulting in political restructuring in the republic. The said situation could be one of the push factors for these entrepreneurs to come to Malaysia.*
>
> (ITE)

> *(I came here) due to the transfer of power in Indonesia. I came to Malaysia to survey the market and look into what kind of opportunities for me to venture into.*
>
> (IME7)

The pull factors within the context of this chapter are mainly the attracting aspects of the host country encouraging IMEs' migration. Given the economic development of Malaysia which is relatively higher than Indonesia, IMEs are pulled into migration in the migrant-receiving country as the host country provides them with employment and entrepreneurial prospects. The pull factors for IMEs pre-1997 and post-1997 are similar in which the respondents explained that the cultural and geographical proximity of Malaysia to Indonesia is one of the main attracting factors to the host country as it reduces the need for learning new markets and new business methods for the respondents. Further, according to our data, cultural similarities reduce IMEs' needs to specifically tailor their products and services to another country's preference, while geographical proximity enables individual and product mobility. This is illustrated by the following comments by a pre-1997 IME, IME9:

> *Malaysia is so near to Indonesia, so accessible, so it was easy for me. I suppose because my parents were concerned that I would get too comfortable living in Indonesia, they asked me to go to Malaysia and look for opportunities. I decided to open a textile business in 1989 because my family is involved in the business back home.*
>
> (IME9)

Several post-1997 IMEs, IME3 (who operates a Malaysia–Indonesia trade venture) and IME4 (who conducts a Balinese spa operation) also explained that Malaysia–Indonesia cultural and geographical proximity are attracting factors for their professional-based migration:

> *The reason why Malaysia was chosen is because of the cultural proximity, distance and also, we have the Indonesians here as our base clients.*
>
> (IME3)

> *Malaysia and Indonesia, we are similar in more ways than one. The food, the language, the culture ... what you wear, what you eat and what you use in daily basis are similar. So the process of adapting to a new market was easier because of that. Then, when it comes to importing and shipment, because of the distance, it will not cost you a bomb. And because of the geographical distance, you can put your shipment in another person's container and it will arrive to you.*
>
> (IME4)

As a country with higher development level than the IMEs' home country, Malaysia is also considered as "a place of opportunity", as clarified by an Indonesian trade association leader, ITE:

> *The situation in Indonesia can be a challenge in operating a business. Malaysia is seen by these entrepreneurs as a place of opportunity ... to start a new life, to start a new business ... There are more opportunities here because of good economic conditions here, and proximity in terms of distance and culture.*
>
> (ITE)

In this aspect based on the evidence, the push factors of emigration largely influence post-1997 IMEs to move to Malaysia, whereas the pull factors that include geographical and cultural closeness encourage them to pursue opportunities in the host country.

Interlinked mechanisms of migration and entrepreneurship activities within the framework of embeddedness

The IMEs were asked about the way migration and entrepreneurial activities were facilitated for them. Responses within this dimension include family and friends in the migrant-receiving country, their employers' arrangements and social passes. In general, professional mechanisms enabling the migration process are largely linked with IMEs' motivation to emigrate; these mechanisms include employment and entrepreneurial aspects. Profession-wise, post-1997 IMEs came to Malaysia as expatriates based on the professional assignments given by their employers in their home country. The expatriate assignments then evolved into entrepreneurship projects which eventually encouraged them to leave their employment to focus on their entrepreneurial ventures in Malaysia. For IMEs who came to Malaysia solely to start a business venture, Malaysia is seen as an opportunity-based market for their established entrepreneurial ventures in Indonesia. When gauged further, the mechanisms under this category are mainly related with IMEs who migrate to Malaysia for opportunity reasons, and they are usually equipped with financial means to survive in the host country, as illustrated in the following quotations by IME4, a spa operator; IME5, a food trader; and ITE, an Indonesian embassy representative:

> *The spa company that I was working for decided to open a branch in Malaysia. That was 1998.*
>
> (IME4)

> *During my tenure as a country manager in Malaysia, I took the time to learn and adapt to the culture in Malaysia, and turns out, there is not much difference.*
>
> (IME5)

> *Some came to Malaysia as labourers, and stayed on and became entrepreneurs.*
>
> (ITE)

Mechanisms enabling migration

For pre-1997 IMEs, personal and institutional mechanisms facilitating the migration process are primarily interrelated with IMEs' personal affiliations in the host country. This category includes aspects such as having friends, close family and long-distance relatives in Malaysia who can assist their migration processes, and facilitated by the institutional arrangements of the migrant-sending and migrant-receiving countries, manifested in the form of social passes. Several narratives within this aspect suggest that the relationships that they have in Malaysia provided them with employment opportunities and living arrangements which are otherwise more difficult to obtain for migrants who do not have any connections in the host country. Consider the following comments by IME1 and an Indonesian association community leader, ICL, regarding their home country social embeddedness in the host country:

> *In terms of settlement, I have received some assistance from my relatives who have moved to Malaysia years before I came here. Also, my uncle has provided me with working experience, by offering me to work in his Jamu business.*
>
> (IME1)

> *Why did I say accessible? Some have long distance relatives here. Some also have acquaintances from their village that have arrived in Malaysia much earlier.*
>
> (ICL)

Post-1997 IMEs' personal mechanisms facilitating the migration process are predominantly interrelated with IMEs' bridging relationships in the host country. IMEs within this category do not have any family members living in Malaysia, unlike pre-1997 IMEs. However, their relationships in the host country are predominantly marriage-based or professional-based. This is illustrated by the experiences of IME5 and IME8. IME5 who conducts a trade venture clarified that her arrival (and the startup of her venture) is facilitated by her previous employment opportunity in Malaysia, while IME8 who manages a restaurant explained that she came to the host country as a result of marriage:

> *I came here as the country manager for Company X, stayed on the job for three years in Malaysia . . . I take it as a learning experience for me. I was learning the system and getting to know the people involved in this business. I also have got the chance to meet Mr Lee, a local, who was the previous owner of this company. He was one of our clients and now he is one of the partners in this business.*
>
> (IME5)

> *To be with my husband . . . My husband mainly has influenced my decision [to migrate and start a business]. When we got married, he asked me what I want to do in Malaysia, I told him that I would like to build a restaurant, so he helped me build it.*
>
> (IME8)

Mechanisms enabling entrepreneurship activities

The theme of intra-regional migration mechanism enabling entrepreneurial activities differs across the two groups. For pre-1997 IMEs, their intra-regional entrepreneurial mechanisms are primarily facilitated by their family members in Malaysia, and, for post-1997 IMEs, their mechanisms are mainly enabled by inexpensive procurement from Indonesia. IME1, a pre-1997 IME, explained that his entrepreneurial venture began after he accumulated business knowledge as a result of working for his uncle in Malaysia, and IME2, who is also a pre-1997 IME, clarified that his family members both in Malaysia and Indonesia have assisted him in developing his logistics venture:

> *I managed my uncle's business two years after I arrived in Malaysia. . . . In 1992, after working with my uncle, I started a small business, very small. With the trust of these manufacturers, I imported their products and sell these products in night markets and directly to consumers. I have received some assistance from my relatives who have moved to Malaysia years before I came here. Also, my uncle has provided me with working experience, by offering me to work in his Jamu business.*
>
> (IME1)

> There is a strong element of family values in this company, as I built this company using the money that I have gained by selling my father's land, and my family, both in Malaysia and Indonesia, helped me a great deal with this company.
>
> (IME2)

Many of the post-1997 IMEs' ventures are facilitated by inexpensive procurement opportunities in Malaysia. Here, IMEs' relations to Indonesia in terms of entrepreneurial framework are largely strategic. Some examples of ventures conducted within this category include procuring teakwood furniture, Balinese spa products and food to be traded in Malaysia. For instance, IME4, a spa operator, clarified that she sourced the products for her operation from her hometown in Bali, and IME7 who conducts a teakwood trade operation explained that he procured the materials for his venture from his hometown, which is one of the premier locations for teakwood supplies in Indonesia. In this way, they are able to source the products in an inexpensive manner and ensure the quality of the procured products based on the trust and relations that they have in their hometowns. Consider the following quotations by IME4 and IME7:

> We only source our products from Bali because I know the market . . . The furniture and wood products, we source them for Bali.
>
> (IME4)

> Our furniture is made from Indonesian teak wood, and made in our manufacturing plant in Indonesia, in my hometown to be exact.
>
> (IME7)

A similar theme across the groups is the role of the Indonesian community in Malaysia; a consistently large number of Indonesians in the host country meant that IMEs are able to leverage on their fellow countrymen as a customer base and a source of inexpensive labour. Some entrepreneurs build their ventures using their fellow countrymen's assistance and utilise them as markets for their ventures. This is exemplified by IME2 and IME6, who are pre-1997 IMEs, and IME3 who represents a post-1997 IME:

> The company was being built under the efforts of Indonesian students in the nearby university; a large part of this company was being contributed by them, in terms of capital and labour . . . We have a strong presence among the Indonesian community in Malaysia . . . mainly with students, as we started off with the help of Indonesian students. We try to sponsor a few of their activities. As for the Indonesian workers, who are our main clients, most of them are return clients, and we are known through word-of-mouth, and other media.
>
> (IME2)

> Right now, we only have Indonesians as our target market . . . specifically Indonesian workers in Malaysia. The bosses of these workers may also be our clients

but then again they contact us because they would like to do something nice for their worker . . . in a sense, almost all of our clients are Indonesian workers.

(IME6)

We have the Indonesians here as our base clients. There is a huge number of Indonesian workers here . . . We came to Malaysia in 1998, started importing to Hong Kong and Vietnam since the last ten years, because we have a huge number of Indonesian workers there, serving us as a market.

(IME3)

Discussion

The investigation of the narratives revealed that there are several similarities and differences for the IMEs from across different waves of migration (pre-1997 IMEs and post-1997 IMEs). In particular, pre-1997 IMEs' migration motivations are based on finding employment and entrepreneurial opportunities, whereas post-1997 motivations are based on professional assignments and the intention to start a new life. Geographical and cultural proximity remain as dominant pull factors for both groups. The mechanisms enabling migration and entrepreneurial endeavours, however, largely differ for the two groups. The narratives were synthesised and displayed using a matrix in Table 5.3.

Table 5.3 Summary of the findings

Subject	Motivation		Migration and entrepreneurial mechanisms	
	Pull factors	*Push factors*	*Mechanisms enabling migration process*	*Mechanisms enabling entrepreneurial activities*
IMEs arriving to Malaysia pre-1997	Geographical proximity Cultural proximity	Finding employment and entrepreneurial opportunities	Family in Malaysia	Family members in Malaysia Indonesians as base customers Indonesians as a labour source
IMEs arriving to Malaysia post-1997	Geographical proximity Cultural proximity	Professional assignment Starting a new life	Marriage Professional ties	Inexpensive procurement from Indonesia Indonesians as base customers Indonesians as a labour source

Embeddedness, geographical and cultural proximities in motivations to migrate

Pre-1997 IMEs, in general, are motivated to emigrate to Malaysia to work, less prepared to start a venture, and their migration processes were enabled by their relatives in the host country. They stayed on and become entrepreneurs, some serving their home countrymen as target markets, while some utilises the similarity between Malaysia and Indonesia to serve the local markets. Post-1997 IMEs, however, are more prepared resource-wise to start a venture in the host country. Most of them are equipped with professional ties in Malaysia as a result of professional working experience in the host country although many of them do not have any personal or family relationships in Malaysia. The varying migration motivations of pre-1997 and post-1997 IMEs are balanced by the geographical and cultural proximities of Malaysia and Indonesia; such proximity encourages trade facilitation and communication for IMEs across the groups thus further enabling their migration and entrepreneurial processes. Here, IMEs are embedded within their intentions and resources in the host country, and such embeddedness is further shaped by the geographical and cultural proximity of Malaysia and Indonesia. In this regard, such aspects provide IMEs with a certain edge against other migrant groups (Weiss & Tulin, in press) but utilised differently according to migrant cohorts. The embeddedness view in migrant entrepreneurship suggests that migrant entrepreneurs' opportunity structure is shaped by the host–home country dynamics (Jones et al., 2014; Kloosterman, 2010; Kloosterman & Rath, 2001). The data of this chapter illustrate that for migrant entrepreneurs migrating within-region, the historical element mainly shapes their experiences thus influencing their motivations and strategies in operating ventures in the host country.

Entrepreneurship activities resulting from home country embeddedness

An emerging theme in the data is the role of the entrepreneurs' home country diaspora community in the migrant-receiving country (Indonesians in Malaysia) as a source of support for IMEs' ventures. Pre-1997 IMEs and post-1997 IMEs show similar qualities within this theme whereby both groups leverage on the Indonesia community in Malaysia as (1) their base customers before moving on to the more lucrative local market and (2) a source of inexpensive labour. The large number of Indonesians in Malaysia could explain this propensity as the size of the Indonesian diaspora community is large enough to form a market and a labour pool. A dimension unavailable in pre-1997 IMEs is post-1997 IMEs' strategic utilisation of their hometowns as a source of inexpensive procurement; some IMEs obtain business supplies and products to be traded in Malaysia from their hometowns, IMEs within this dimension clarified that this procurement process is further enabled by trust, as they personally know the people involved.

From the data, the mechanisms enabling IMEs' migration to Malaysia and their ventures are largely composed of professional, personal and institutional explanatory dimensions. Based on the different characteristics of such mechanisms from the findings, it can be suggested that historical contexts mainly influence migrants' motivations and strategies in the host country. Migrants as individuals experience time and environment in accordance to the historical social and political contexts, as their well-being in their home countries are largely affected by the changes in their home nations. Here, the socially constructed nature of time (Bluedorn & Standifer, 2006) shapes individuals' (in this case migrants) experiences in a specific situation (Ancona et al., 2001; Kim et al., 2019).

Cultural similarity, geographical proximity, home country population and historical contexts for Indonesian migrant entrepreneurs

Indonesia–Malaysia cultural similarities, which mainly covers similarity in language and shared history enables IMEs' communication in the host country, product knowledge and preferences. The two countries' geographical proximity, however, encourages mobility for products and individuals. Such proximity attributes to a large home country-based population in the host country, which further enables activation of personal networks and providing IMEs with a customer base and labour source. Cultural similarities, geographical proximity and a large number of home country population in the host country consistently act as facilitating factors for migration and entrepreneurship for IMEs in Malaysia for both cohorts. However, a comparison of two migrant cohorts in the host nation shows that historical contexts could attribute to IMEs' migration and venture strategies in the host country. The embeddedness of the migration and entrepreneurial activities shaped by cultural similarity, geographical proximity and historical aspects for this chapter is illustrated in Figure 5.2.

Conclusions

This chapter contributes to the discussion of embeddedness in migration by examining IMEs' migration motives and enabling mechanisms in Malaysia, outlined by the embeddedness framework (Jack & Anderson, 2002; Uzzi, 1997). The types of migrants received by Malaysia are largely for the purpose of labour, especially in low-skilled sectors such as construction and domestic services. Theory-wise, this chapter suggests that embeddedness can be more salient in intra-regional contexts especially when historical dimension is taken into account. More importantly, this chapter indicates that although the motivation to migrate and their entrepreneurial focus differ (less strategic versus more strategic), pre-1997 and post-1997 IMEs are enabled by (1) the Malaysia–Indonesia cultural and geographical proximity and (2) the large number of Indonesians in Malaysia. Practice-wise, the consistent role of Indonesia–Malaysia cultural and geographical proximity and the large population of home country population in the

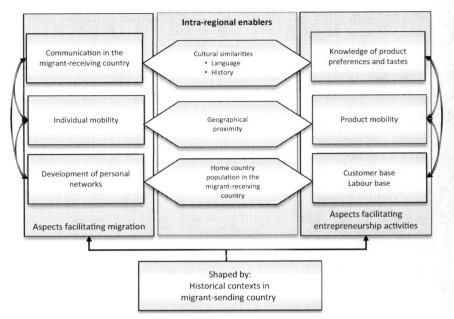

Figure 5.2 The embeddedness of the migration and entrepreneurial activities

host country provides a structure for future entrepreneurial opportunities for entrepreneurs between the two countries. In contrast to the traditional view of ethnic migrant entrepreneurship where the home country market is considered unprofitable, a large home country population could mean otherwise for ethnic migrant entrepreneurs. Additionally, the proximities shared by the two countries imply that little to no modifications are needed when it comes to marketing and business for locals. The narratives illustrate that the trajectory towards business ownership in a close, neighbouring country for Indonesian entrepreneurs is multi-dimensional; a result of various push and pull factors enabled by layers of migration-facilitating mechanisms and embeddedness. As such, skilled migrants can utilise this framework as a guiding model to navigate their mobility within the region.

This chapter investigated Indonesian entrepreneurs who migrate to Malaysia who develop and operate entrepreneurial ventures. This chapter's findings indicate that within-migration experience is beyond "searching for a better life", in which migrants are embedded within layers of ties and relations to their home countries, especially if the sending and receiving countries are geographically and culturally proximate. As such, this chapter illuminates Indonesian entrepreneurship from the perspective of migrant entrepreneurship and practice-wise, the findings of this chapter will be valuable for policymakers in Indonesia especially within the areas of international labour and trade.

Although limited by the context of IMEs in Malaysia, this chapter's findings demonstrate that intra-regional migration will see a more dynamic landscape beyond labour-based migration. As this chapter is particularly focused on Southeast Asia, perhaps future research can consider studying the aspects shaping intra-regional migrant entrepreneurship in other geographical regions, using historical accounts and narratives.

References

Abd Hamid, H., Everett, A. M., & O'Kane, C. (2018). Ethnic migrant entrepreneurs' opportunity exploitation and cultural distance: A classification through a matrix of opportunities. *Asian Academy of Management Journal, 23*(1), 151–169.

Abd Hamid, H., O'Kane, C., & Everett, A. M. (2019). Conforming to the host country versus being distinct to our home countries: Ethnic migrant entrepreneurs' identity work in cross-cultural settings. *International Journal of Entrepreneurial Behavior & Research, 25*(5), 919–935.

Abel, G. J., Raymer, J., & Guan, Q. (2019). Driving factors of Asian international migration flows. *Asian Population Studies, 15*(3), 243–265.

Aliaga-Isla, R., & Rialp, A. (2013). Systematic review of immigrant entrepreneurship literature: Previous findings and ways forward. *Entrepreneurship & Regional Development, 25*(9–10), 819–844.

Ancona, D. G., Okhuysen, G. A., & Perlow, L. A. (2001). Taking time to integrate temporal research. *Academy of Management Review, 26*(4), 512–529.

Anggadwita, G., Luturlean Bachruddin, S., Ramadani, V., & Ratten, V. (2017). Sociocultural environments and emerging economy entrepreneurship: Women entrepreneurs in Indonesia. *Journal of Entrepreneurship in Emerging Economies, 9*(1), 85–96.

Arifin, E. N., Ananta, A., Wilujeng Wahyu Utami, D. R., Budi Handayani, N., & Pramono, A. (2015). Quantifying Indonesia's ethnic diversity. *Asian Population Studies, 11*(3), 233–256.

Barrett, R., & Vershinina, N. (2017). Intersectionality of ethnic and entrepreneurial identities: A study of post-war Polish entrepreneurs in an English city. *Journal of Small Business Management, 55*(3), 430–443.

Bastide, L. (in press). Incorporating transnational labour: Migration rent, combined relocation, and offshore production networks in Malaysia. *Migration Studies*.

Bluedorn, A. C., & Standifer, R. L. (2006). Time and the temporal imagination. *Academy of Management Learning & Education, 5*(2), 196–206.

Carter, S., Mwaura, S., Ram, M., Trehan, K., & Jones, T. (2015). Barriers to ethnic minority and women's enterprise: Existing evidence, policy tensions and unsettled questions. *International Small Business Journal, 33*(1), 49–69.

De Haas, H. (2010). Migration and development: A theoretical perspective. *International Migration Review, 44*(1), 227–264.

Denzin, N. K., & Lincoln, Y. S. (Eds.). (2011). *The Sage handbook of qualitative research* (4th ed.). Thousand Oaks, CA: Sage Publications.

Erel, U., & Ryan, L. (2019). Migrant capitals: Proposing a multi-level spatio-temporal analytical framework. *Sociology, 53*(2), 246–263.

Essers, C., Benschop, Y., & Doorewaard, H. (2010). Female ethnicity: Understanding Muslim immigrant businesswomen in the Netherlands. *Gender, Work & Organization, 17*(3), 320–339.

Flyvbjerg, B. (2006). Five misunderstandings about case-study research. *Qualitative Inquiry*, 12(2), 219–245.

Gamlen, A., Cummings, M. E., & Vaaler, P. M. (2019). Explaining the rise of diaspora institutions. *Journal of Ethnic and Migration Studies*, 45(4), 492–516.

Hasanah, T. (2015). Potential social capital of Indonesian immigrant in Malaysia: A preliminary research. *Procedia-Social and Behavioral Sciences*, 211, 383–389.

Hugo, G. (2005). The new international migration in Asia. *Asian Population Studies*, 1(1), 93–120.

Hugo, G. (2014). A multi sited approach to analysis of destination immigration data: An Asian example. *International Migration Review*, 48(4), 998–1027.

Jack, S. L., & Anderson, A. R. (2002). The effects of embeddedness on the entrepreneurial process. *Journal of Business Venturing*, 17(5), 467–487.

Jamaludin, N. A., Senik, Z. C., Abd Hamid, H., & Muhamad, N. S. a. (2020). Opportunity recognition in immigrant entrepreneurship through social capital and geographical proximity: A conceptual framework. *Geografia: Malaysian Journal of Society and Space*, 16(3).

Jones, T., Ram, M., Edwards, P., Kiselinchev, A., & Muchenje, L. (2014). Mixed embeddedness and new migrant enterprise in the UK. *Entrepreneurship & Regional Development*, 26(5–6), 500–520.

Kaur, A. (2004). *Mobility, labor migration and border controls: Indonesian labor migration to Malaysia since 1900*. Paper presented at the 15th Biennial Conference of the Asian Studies Association of Australia, Canberra, Australia. Retrieved on 10th May 2021, from http://coombs.anu.edu.au/SpecialProj/ASAA/biennial-conference/2004/Kaur-A-ASAA2004.pdf.

Kaur, A. (2008). International migration and governance in Malaysia: Policy and performance. *UNEAC Asia Papers*, 22, 4–18.

Khalid, K. M., & Yacob, S. (2012). Managing Malaysia – Indonesia relations in the context of democratization: The emergence of non-state actors. *International Relations of the Asia-Pacific*, 12(3), 355–387.

Kim, A., Bansal, P., & Haugh, H. M. (2019). No time like the present: How a present time perspective can foster sustainable development. *Academy of Management Journal*, 62(2), 607–634.

Kloosterman, R. C. (2010). Matching opportunities with resources: A framework for analysing (migrant) entrepreneurship from a mixed embeddedness perspective. *Entrepreneurship & Regional Development*, 22(1), 25–45.

Kloosterman, R. C., & Rath, J. (2001). Immigrant entrepreneurs in advanced economies: Mixed embeddedness further explored. *Journal of Ethnic and Migration Studies*, 27(2), 189–201.

Koning, J., & Verver, M. (2013). Historicizing the 'ethnic' in ethnic entrepreneurship: The case of the ethnic Chinese in Bangkok. *Entrepreneurship & Regional Development*, 25(5–6), 325–348.

Liow, J. C. (2005a). *The politics of Indonesia-Malaysia relations: One kin, two nations*. Oxon, UK: RoutledgeCurzon.

Liow, J. C. (2005b). Tunku Abdul Rahman and Malaya's relations with Indonesia, 1957–1960. *Journal of Southeast Asian Studies*, 36(1), 87–109.

Marsden, P. V. (1981). Introducing influence processes into a system of collective decisions. *American Journal of Sociology*, 86(6), 1203–1235.

McKeever, E., Jack, S., & Anderson, A. (2015). Embedded entrepreneurship in the creative re-construction of place. *Journal of Business Venturing*, 30(1), 50–65.

Miles, M. B., & Huberman, M. A. (1994). *Qualitative data analysis: An expanded sourcebook*. Thousand Oaks, CA: Sage Publications.

Mosbah, A., Debili, R., & Merazga, H. (2018). First-generation immigrant entrepreneurship in Malaysia: What do we know so far? *Kasetsart Journal of Social Sciences*, 39(2), 351–357.

Munandar, A. S. (2003). Culture and management in Indonesia. In M. Warner (Ed.), *Culture and management in Asia* (pp. 82–98). London, UK: RoutledgeCurzon.

Ozdemir, S. Z., Moran, P., Zhong, X., & Bliemel, M. J. (2016). Reaching and acquiring valuable resources: The entrepreneur's use of brokerage, cohesion, and embeddedness. *Entrepreneurship Theory and Practice*, 40(1), 49–79.

Peters, N. (2002). Mixed embeddedness: Does it really explain immigrant enterprise in Western Australia (WA)? *Journal of Entrepreneurial Behaviour and Research*, 8(1–2), 32–53.

Rahman, M. M., & Fee, L. K. (2009). Gender and the remittance process: Indonesian domestic workers in Hong Kong, Singapore and Malaysia. *Asian Population Studies*, 5(2), 103–125.

Ram, M., Theodorakopoulos, N., & Jones, T. (2008). Forms of capital, mixed embeddedness and Somali enterprise. *Work, Employment and Society*, 22(3), 427–446.

Rodgers, P., Vershinina, N., Williams, C. C., & Theodorakopoulos, N. (2019). Leveraging symbolic capital: The use of blat networks across transnational spaces. *Global Networks*, 19(1), 119–136.

Spaan, E., & van Naerssen, T. (2018). Migration decision-making and migration industry in the Indonesia – Malaysia corridor. *Journal of Ethnic and Migration Studies*, 44, 680–695.

Storti, L. (2014). Being an entrepreneur: Emergence and structuring of two immigrant entrepreneur groups. *Entrepreneurship & Regional Development*, 26(7–8), 521–545.

United Nations. (2019). Trends in international migrant stock: Migrants by destination and origin. *Department of Economic and Social Affairs*. Retrieved on 10th May 2021, from www.un.org/en/development/desa/population/migration/data/estimates2/estimates19.asp.

Uzzi, B. (1997). Social structure and competition in interfirm networks: The paradox of embeddedness. *Administrative Science Quarterly*, 42(1), 35–67.

Weiss, A., & Tulin, M. (in press). Does mentoring make immigrants more desirable? A conjoint analysis. *Migration Studies*.

Wong, D. (2006). The recruitment of foreign labor in Malaysia: From migration system to guest worker regime. In A. Kaur & I. Metcalfe (Eds.), *Mobility, labor migration, and border controls in Asia* (pp. 211–227). Basingstoke, UK: Palgrave Macmillan.

World Bank. (2017). *World migration report*. Geneva, Switzerland: World Bank.

World Bank. (2019). *World development indicators*. Retrieved on 10th May 2021, from https://datacatalog.worldbank.org/dataset/world-development-indicators.

Yin, R. K. (2014). *Case study research: Design and methods* (5th ed.). Thousand Oaks, CA: Sage Publications.

6 Technology entrepreneurship in Indonesia

Vanessa Ratten

Introduction

Digital transformation is a market process that has the potential to significantly change business practices (Apostolopoulos et al., 2020). Digitalisation is complex as it involves creating new electronic applications that further advance the internet economy. Cutting-edge technology is technology that includes new forms of technological innovation into its products, services or processes (Ratten, 2020a). The use of cutting-edge technology has revolutionised industries and spurred entrepreneurship. As a result, technological innovation is increasingly being used in entrepreneurial endeavours. Emerging technologies are changing the way individuals and businesses interact in society (Ratten, 2020b). The most well-known cutting-edge technologies include artificial intelligence, augmented reality, virtual reality, wearable technology, robots and big data analytics (Ameen, Hosany, & Tarhini, in press).

New technologies are revolutionising marketing communications as they provide more personalised services. This is having profound effects on the way customers interact with companies by providing a more interactive process. Virtual reality refers to a technology environment that can or cannot mimic the real world. This, in turn, is enabling a better experience for consumers that takes into account real time information. New technology in the form of data analytics has enabled information to be accessed in real time. This enables huge amounts of information to be obtained that can provide directions on human behaviour. By using this data to predict events, it can lead to time efficiencies. Artificial intelligence refers to the use of technology to make computers do certain tasks. This involves imitating human behaviour through computers. Increasingly the use of artificial intelligence is being promoted in society in order to provide consumer insights. This is due to the way technology can use predictive analytics to analyse current and future behaviour, thereby enhancing customer experiences by encompassing emotional and social intelligence. The goal of this chapter is to discuss the way technology innovation is utilised in Indonesia. To do this, a discussion of the role of technology unicorns in Indonesia is stated. This helps to understand why innovation is needed in the Indonesian economy.

DOI: 10.4324/9781003187769-6

Technology unicorns in Indonesia

A unicorn is a startup that has a valuation of $1 billion or more. The most well-known unicorns in Indonesia are Go-Jek, Traveloka, Bukalapak and Tokopedia. Go-Jek is an on-demand and multi-service platform originally developed as a ride-hailing service. Since its launch in 2015, it has diversified into an app service providing more than 20 services. This includes ride sharing, shopping and food delivery services. It is considered as one of the most successful Indonesian startups and was the first unicorn company in the country. The name Go-Jek derives from the word 'ojek' which refers to motorbike taxis that are common in Southeast Asia. In order to expand its online payment business, it has acquired other fintech firms. Go-Jek has expanded its business to the Philippines, Singapore, Thailand and Vietnam. Go-Jek has a number of other products that all have the 'Go' name. This includes Go-Pay, an electronic wallet service; Go-Car, a car hailing service; and Go-Mart, a grocery shopping service. Other notable products include Go-Clean a cleaning service and Go-Tix an electronic ticketing service. Go-Jek has more than 2 million driver partners and 900,000 food merchant partners. Go-Jek now has three major platforms: consumer, driver and merchant applications. Go-Jek provides an electronic ecosystem that supports the growth of entrepreneurial firms. This has been particularly helpful during the Covid-19 pandemic with more consumers and businesses requiring online systems.

Traveloka is an online ticket and hotel booking service. It initially focused on accommodation and flight bookings but has expanded to include food features, home protection insurance, movie booking and visa insurance. Its main market is Indonesia but it also serves Malaysia, Thailand, Philippines, Vietnam, Singapore and Australia. The website started as a way to compare airline ticket prices but then started selling airline tickets.

Bukalapak is an e-commerce company that acts as an online marketplace for enterprises to go online. It started in 2010 as a way of enabling businesses to sell their goods online. The online environment enables small and medium-sized enterprises to broaden the market. Due to the large number of consumers in Indonesia, Bukalapak enables a way of bridging the gap between buyer and seller. The aim of the company is to help Indonesia's micro-economy to be competitive. To do this, businesses advertise their services on an e-commerce platform. Tokopedia is a technology company that specialises in e-commerce. It started as a marketplace business that has since grown to a financial technology company.

Technology innovation

Startups are major economic creators and play a key role in fostering entrepreneurship. Newly established businesses in the form of startups are expected to increase economic development but at the same time be cognisant of social and environmental obligations. Entrepreneurship is an indispensable part of any economy. New types of customers have emerged on digital platforms due to the growth in unofficial businesses. Digital platforms are defined as "a set of digital resources- including services and content- that enable value-creating interactions between external producers and consumers" (Constantinides, Henfridsson, & Parker, 2018: 381). These businesses are usually in the form of startup enterprises that are established to fill a certain market need. Often these unofficial businesses are informal in nature and can respond to rapid change in demand. This makes them nimble and open to new market opportunities.

The word 'innovation' is considered a golden term to describe positive change. This means that innovation can be misunderstood due to its elusiveness. Whilst innovation as a concept is commonly used in society, its definition refers to a broad concept that is dynamic in nature. This results in the way innovation is understood by an individual being based on their mindset. Individuals with a progressive view on innovation view it as a necessity to producing a better society. Individuals who are happy with current conditions and the status quo may view innovation as being a costly and time-wasting activity. This is due to innovation sometimes requiring some form of risk as the outcome of the change is unknown. This means that special resources may be needed to evaluate the potential of an innovative idea.

Innovation does not necessarily mean something that is completely new as it can involve the rediscovery of previous behaviours or include the introduction of reconfigured behaviour. However, normally innovation involves the introduction of something new into society. This can include an idea, process or method depending on the situation. The capacity of an entity to be innovative is called innovativeness. Innovation implies there is a good outcome from a change. Innovation needs to be considered in a holistic manner as it represents different types of activity. Some technology providers are more innovative than others due to the kind of technology they are involved in. For example, emerging technology is based on risk-taking activity, so it needs to keep up to date with societal conditions. Other technology providers due to their large market share and position in the marketplace do not have to be innovative. This is due to some forms of technology such as cultural technology being based on historical conditions that are not likely to change. Due to the emphasis in society on technological innovation, there has been a tendency to assume all innovation as being technologically based. This is not always the case as innovation can be related to a changing mindset. Therefore, innovation whilst often involving technology can also refer to alternations in existing assumptions. This paves the way for new ways of thinking to emerge that challenge the status quo.

Innovation is hard work as it takes time to develop. This means not all innovation happens overnight but rather is the accumulation of a lot of effort. To induce innovation, there needs to be the right processes in place to make it happen. This means establishing clear goals and reviewing progress at every step. This will enable an innovative idea to come to fruition. Innovation needs to be managed in the same way other processes are in order to make sure it occurs in the right way. Most of the innovative ideas come from recognising an opportunity in the marketplace that others have not seen. Therefore, persistence is needed at the initial stages of an innovation in order to overcome market resistance. Once the innovation has become recognised as a good idea, it is then easier to manage. An innovation differs from other business functions due to it being an idea or source of knowledge. Thus, other business activities involve doing whereas innovation focuses on knowing something of value. Astute business managers value innovation as it can give them a competitive advantage. However, recognising an innovation then converting it into an opportunity can take time. Innovation arises from a realisation that there is an opportunity in the marketplace. The inspiration for an innovation can come from a variety of places including experience or expert knowledge. Therefore, innovation enables existing or new resources to be used for wealth creation purposes.

Successful innovations often do not last long in the marketplace before they are replaced by other innovations. Therefore, it is important to build and maintain an innovation in order to keep its competitiveness. To do this requires an innovation strategy, which refers to a plan of action regarding an innovation. Having an innovation strategy in place can help prevent negative events from occurring. This is useful as a risk management strategy and to alleviate concerns. Good innovation strategies engage in forecasting scenarios about potential causes of action. This helps in clarifying priorities and objectives about an innovation. To do this requires a well thought-out plan that emphasises the future needs. An innovation strategy requires the integration of a number of systems that are interlinked. These systems synthesise ideas and help progress an innovation. An innovation system presents a set of structures that can select which direction to take. This involves making trade-off decisions and weighing up different paths to take.

Innovativeness is a skill valued and increasingly being taught in society. Innovation involves some form of change normally of a positive nature. Increasingly innovation is being used as a buzzword to describe creativity. This means that the emphasis is on renewal or modifications to existing behaviour. In order to stimulate economic growth, innovation is required. It helps to move on from the past and think about future occurrences. It can be difficult to describe innovation as it takes on a variety of different forms, which means that innovation is contextual as it depends on the circumstances. Innovation is based on the capacity of an individual or entity to accept change. This means that there can be some ambiguity as to how the innovation evolves in the marketplace. Novelty or newness is at the heart of any conceptualisation of innovation. This means that the change results from a departure or alteration from existing practices.

There is a tendency to describe innovation in a binary way such as good or bad, incremental or radical, or evolutionary or revolutionary. This distinction makes it easier to understand but limits how innovation occurs in society. Therefore, innovation whilst existing in a continuum from small to large change also occurs as a process. This means that innovation can occur quickly but often is the result of a number of different steps. Each step provides a source of knowledge for an entity to learn about how to improve. Innovation is based on demand and represents a source of competitiveness.

Creativity is essential for any form of innovation. This is due to the need to rethink current practices by involving a problem-solving approach. Powerful new ideas that emerge in society are based on societal needs. This means creative thinking is required in order to bring about innovation. Innovation is associated with invention but is more than invention as it focuses on the business applications of invention. The main types of innovation are product, process and service-based. Typically, product innovations refer to changes in tangible goods, whilst process innovation refers to the time taken to conduct an action being altered. More recently, service innovations have been emphasised due to the increased number of intangible transactions occurring in society. The knowledge economy and resulting digital transformation have emphasised service innovations.

Innovation is a form of dynamic capability as it enables actions needed to modify behaviour. The dynamism or flexibility is important as the change can occur in a number of ways. Organisations are seeking to be innovative by modifying their existing operations in order to be more competitive. By looking at an existing situation in a new way, it can enable new results to emerge. This alternative way of thinking is useful particularly when new contexts emerge in the marketplace.

Types of technology innovation

At the heart of most studies on technology, innovation is how to create and sustain wealth creation. Technology innovation is a word that appears frequently since it is important in understanding technology business growth. There are a variety of ways to analyse technology innovation but few explicitly define its usage. Moreover, when researchers seldom do define technology innovation normally they use a simplistic approach without considering its complex nature. This makes it difficult to generalise research as whilst there are many research studies they are analysing it in a different way. In order to build a comprehensive body of research on technology innovation, a number of studies are required but there also needs to be some degree of comparability.

An opportunity in a technology context can involve an idea or project that is currently not under consideration by others. Opportunities can be found in the marketplace by identifying needs. These needs can be in existence or are futuristic in nature. In order to assess an opportunity, there needs to be a discovery process. This means finding solutions to unmet expectations that exist in society. To do this is a cognitive process as it requires counterfactual thinking. Technology innovation involves recognising opportunities by focusing on purposeful change that can lead to a benefit in the market. Innovation results from a conscious effort to try new things. This means within each innovation is a sense of curiosity as to what the idea will produce. Innovation can arise from unexpected occurrences or situations that require new thinking. Furthermore, market changes can lead to an innovation taking place. In times of economic turmoil, innovations can take on a societal function in terms of enabling more members of society access to a service. In good economic conditions, the innovation may lead to more financial gain in terms of obtaining additional revenue. Moreover, as there has been an increased usage of technology in the market changes in socio-demographic behaviour require new products or services. This makes innovation useful in order to fill the gap in the market from technological advancement.

Innovations sometimes have unexpected success with the original idea altered based on market feedback. Thus, it is important with all forms of innovation to obtain feedback. This enables innovations to metamorphise into other types of products that suit specific market needs. Failure is part of innovation as it can take numerous iterations of an innovation to result in a successful outcome. Innovations can initially be disregarded by others due to their unknown nature. This makes it important to stress the usefulness of an innovation then to educate others about its role in the market. Some individuals may dismiss innovations as being a bad idea as they are comfortable with the status quo. This means that current market practices may be preferred due to the substantial amount of resources invested.

Innovations can have unanticipated possibilities that lead to further innovations. An initial innovation may fall fort of expectations and require further adaptations. This means that it is useful to think of an innovation as a continual and dynamic process that changes based on need. Innovation requires ingenuity in terms of thinking creatively to see possibilities. This means focusing one's attention on future market trends to identify gaps in the market. Purposeful innovation requires skill. This refers to being innovative is a process that can be learnt over time. Individuals who persist and overcome hurdles are likely to be more innovative. This is important in today's competitive global marketplace when differentiating your product from others is important. Innovation takes time and diligence in obtaining a good outcome. Businesses need to adapt due to changing government regulations and technology requirements. Thus, it is important that businesses think about the future in anticipating change.

Innovation needs to be adopted as part of a business life in order to create value. Once an innovation is successful, there can be a risk that a sense of complacency results. This can be damaging to the innovation as competitors come into the marketplace and copy their idea. Therefore, continual learning and acquiring new knowledge about marketplace changes are needed. Sustained innovation over a long time period is needed in order to cope with change. Managing current market conditions with future needs can be difficult. Therefore, businesses need to have highly effective learning systems to make this happen. Improving on today's innovation whilst preparing for tomorrow is a skill. This is important as businesses evolve and more knowledge about an innovation becomes known.

Innovation is associated with major technological and global advances such as the introduction of mobile commerce systems. Although most of the innovations are based on cumulative incremental innovations that take time to develop, innovation also involves the creative combination of new skills that can be utilised in the market. Incremental innovations are small changes to existing products or services. They normally provide extensions or additional features that add value. Incremental innovations occur all the time and are often derived from customer requirements. Disruptive innovation involves any form of substantial ongoing change. This means that the disruption caused by innovation takes on a risk-taking nature as there is a threat that the effort will result in negative consequences. Thus, disruptive innovations need to be analysed in a holistic manner taking into account both short- and long-term consequences. This enables the short-term reactive reaction to be softened by more longer-term positive outcomes. Disruptive innovation has a tendency to shake up an industry by introducing fundamental change. This can make it difficult for existing firms to keep up to date with new change.

Kahn (2018) suggests that the main types of product innovation are cost reductions, product improvements, line extensions, new markets, new uses, new category entries and new to the world products. Cost reductions enable cheaper prices to be paid for products. This can involve the use of new materials or methods that lower the cost of production. Product improvements involve enhancements to products that increase a product's value in the marketplace. To do this, new features might be added to a product in order to increase its usability. This enhances its usefulness in the market and attracts customers. The main characteristic of product improvements is that the product is better than before. Line extensions involve adding new options to an existing product. This can include complementary services to those that are already in existence in the marketplace. Additional product offerings help increase a products marketability. New markets involve finding new usages for a product. This can include alternative ways to use the product or the entry into new geographic markets. New uses involve positioning products for different usages. This enables new forms of products to emerge that have additional functions. New categories involve making products that suit an additional market segment. This can include a previously unknown market segment that emerges due to technological innovation. New to the world products are completely new products that have not been seen before. They can emerge from technological developments that enable ideas to become a reality.

Innovation is critical to tourism development and enables new business models to emerge in the marketplace. Regions with no tradition of attracting visitors can be transformed with the use of innovative strategies. Entrepreneurship provides many opportunities for innovation both in the formal and informal sectors. The formal technology sector includes activities that are registered as technology services such as web services. The informal technology sector is not officially identified as being a technology provider but rather exists in an informal manner. Entrepreneurship involves creating novel products or services that have not been identified previously in the marketplace. These novel ideas are implemented in a creative way. Innovation involves perceived new ideas. The idea might not be new but its perception as being different makes it new in the current context. Contemporary technology owes its origins to pioneering innovators that transformed the industry.

Collaborative innovation provides a way for firms to tap into other firms' resources (Feranita, Kotlar, & De Massis, 2017). This is useful in terms of gaining additional knowledge and insight from other sources. Feranita et al. (2017: 138) define collaborative innovation as "a form of inter-firm relationship that involves the exchange and sharing of resources such as financial capital, information, knowledge and technology with external parties in order to achieve innovation". There is increased emphasis on collaboration due to firms realising they cannot do everything themselves. This means that firms can leverage on others to obtain the necessary support for innovation purposes. Collaborative innovation involves embracing an open culture to the sharing of information. This is important as obtaining information in a timely manner can influence the success of an innovation.

It is hard to determine what role institutions play in innovation. This is due to innovation resulting from a number of different factors that produce new ideas. Techno-economic innovations involve technology being used in a more effective way in order to promote economic efficiency. Regulatory innovations are defined as innovations that "transform explicit regulations and/or the ways they are sanctioned" (Heiskala, 2007: 59). Increasingly more emphasis in society is being placed on efficiency with the move from a paper to online based system. This means regulatory authorities have tried to introduce innovation in order to make it easier to use services. This includes the use of self-service technology as a form of regulatory and user innovation. Normative innovations are defined as innovations that "challenge established value commitments and/or the way the values are specified into legitimate social norms" (Heiskala, 2007: 59). These normative innovations can include dress standards or ways of behaving in society.

Increasingly changes in societal conduct are based on the increased usage of technological innovation. Mobile phone technology has resulted in the introduction of video calls that have changed the nature of communication. This has led to alterations in the way people interact, which is a social norm. Cultural innovations are defined as innovations that "challenge the established ways to interpret reality by transforming mental paradigms, cognitive frames and habits of interpretations" (Heiskala, 2007: 59). This form of innovation is also largely based around technological change and the way individuals perceive cultural change.

Open innovation is a type of innovation that has gained popularity because of the increased interest in co-creation activities. Chesbrough (2003: 43) defined open innovation as the process whereby "valuable ideas can come from inside or outside the company and can go to market from inside or outside the company as well". This definition stresses the free-flowing nature of innovation and how it can be helpful to obtain the input from multiple stakeholders. In the past, it was considered better to limit the amount of information about an innovation that was shared with others. With the introduction of the internet and increased online capabilities, the need to share information has increased.

Online communities

Increasingly online rather than physical communities are influencing people's behaviour. The ease and quickness of communication online have further fuelled the growth of online communication. Online communities are defined as "social aggregations that emerge from the Net when enough people carry on those public discussions long enough, with sufficient human feeling, to form webs of personal relationships in cyberspace" (Rheingold, 1993: 7). With more people having access to mobile communication, it is becoming easier to communicate with others regardless of location. People like to form communities online as a form of social support and to exchange information. There are other reasons why the number of online communities has grown and this includes entertainment value and recreation. Thus, people utilise online communities as a source of self-discovery that leads to the accumulation of knowledge. This enhances interpersonal connectivity.

Online environments enable groups to be formed in both a planned and adhoc manner. This enables people to come together and form a community based on a common interest. The need of individuals to belong to a community has motivated them to join online formats. These communities act as a source of support and help shape group members views of a topic. The connections that individuals form online enables them to form connections. These connections are a valuable source of knowledge and value. In an online community, individuals can transfer knowledge and learn from others. This provides a sense of value co-creation and enhances long-term goals.

New markets are being created all the time due to the emergence of different products and solutions. Sprong, Driessen, Hillebrand and Molner (in press: 1) define a market innovation as "purposive action by market stakeholders that result in a distinctively new or altered form of market". This has led to changing market structures and altered market behaviour. As a result, businesses have had to change how they interact with their stakeholders. Market innovation is a political and social process as it requires institutional change. Therefore, to create a new market involves receiving the input of stakeholders in terms of resource acquisition and exchange (Huarng & Yu, in press).

Customer entrepreneurship

In the increasingly connected digital world, customer entrepreneurship is becoming more prevalent. Customer entrepreneurship is defined as "the entrepreneurial activities of actors conventionally categorised as end-consumers or end-users in ecosystems" (Park, Kim, Jeong, & Minshall, 2021: 96). This is altering the position of customers on digital platforms from end-users to more active participants. This is resulting in business model innovation as customers become more active about pursuing innovation. Customers are normally viewed as target audiences rather than innovators. This means traditionally customers are the buyers of products or services rather than co-creators. This role has changed with customers being proactive entrepreneurs on digital platforms. Increasingly customers are trading goods online with the goal of making a profit. This has led to goods being sold online in advance then being resold in other online platforms. The volume of this online trade is considerable and effects the international market. Customer entrepreneurs are normally everyday people using platforms for business activities. The platforms increasingly are digital based but they can also be through traditional mechanisms such as bricks and mortar shops. Normally the customer entrepreneurs operate their business as a side project and have another main business. In order to maximise profits, customer entrepreneurs use social media and other marketing activities. Customer entrepreneurs constantly appraise their performance by evaluating the market. This involves focusing on pricing adjustments and advertising strategies. When the market or demand is shifting, customers can decrease prices. Due to the informal and friendship-based nature of customer entrepreneurs, their market transactions tend to be small. This leads to an emphasis on word of mouth or direct marketing for sales. Unlike professional and full-time entrepreneurs, the commercial activities of customer entrepreneurs tend to occur on an ad hoc basis. This makes the purchase decisions based on access to the products.

Price is an important determinant of consumers decision to buy a product. Consumers normally are more price sensitive with online purchases as they have time to shop around. This makes it important for online stores to make it easy to search for products. This will impact the degree of loyalty consumers have towards a brand. Those with channel loyalty will repurchase items from their preferred channels. This makes it important for online retailers to emphasise customer loyalty through their websites. Technological literacy is defined as "individual capabilities to use technology such as digital devices and software, in various areas of life" (Park et al., 2021: 103). Some individuals have a higher level of technological literacy than others due to their ability to integrate technology into their lifestyle. This enables individuals to interact with technology particularly that of a digital kind. Individuals need to trust that the technology is reliable and safe. This means that they have confidence in the integrity and usefulness of the technology.

Technology marketing

Marketing is a process that involves making then keeping promises to consumers (Grönroos, 2006). This means that there is a sense of obligation inherent in any form of marketing communication. Shaw (2012: 31) states "marketing covers an entire discipline that contains both micro (e.g. marketing management, buyer behaviour and consumer psychology) and macro (e.g. industry, distribution channels and aggregate marketing system) perspectives". Marketing strategy involves planning for the future in terms of anticipating demand. Normally whether this obligation has been met is determined by the perceptions of a consumer. This means that there is some degree of subjectivity as to whether the goals of a marketing campaign have been achieved. Marketing is an essential part of any economy as it enables producers of goods to advertise their services. The general perception of marketing has tended to be negative due to the large amount of money businesses spend on marketing. This means that marketing is sometimes stereotyped as an advantageous activity that biases large businesses that have the financial resources to afford to do so. Moreover, marketers have been stereotyped as salespeople that over exaggerate the usefulness of a product. This has led to marketers being viewed as unauthentic. Whilst this stereotype has changed with the advance of new marketing campaigns based on direct interaction between buyer and seller, there is still some negative connotations.

The 4Ps of marketing involve product, price, promotion and place. In a technology context, the product means what actual goods or services are exchanged. The price is also important due to some technology providers competing on price whilst others being price inelastic. Promotion can occur in a variety of ways including through social media, direct advertising or traditional marketing mechanisms such as word of mouth or print media.

Marketing is essentially an exchange process based on the perception of value. This means that, when marketing occurs, it is the result of some form of exchange. The exchange can be transactional in terms of a specific time frame or of a continual nature. Increasingly relationships are being utilised in technology transactions due to the need to include the input of many different stakeholders. Relationship marketing is defined as "attracting, maintaining and-in-multi-service organisations- enhancing customer relationships" (Berry, 1983: 25). Relationship technology marketers develop segmentation strategies to suit different markets. This makes technology marketing fundamentally about understanding the customers in a business relationship then building strategies with them in order to maintain the relationship. This means that marketing is a broad set of activities and processes that facilitate communication about offerings. This communication can occur in a direct or indirect way depending on the context. In order to enable the communication, information about the offerings needs to be exchanged. The information enables marketers to monitor marketing performance and to re-evaluate actions, thereby generating new solutions that can further create more value.

There are a number of different types of marketing with new types emerging constantly in the marketplace. Relationship marketing refers to strategies that encourage loyalty to be built between the buyer and seller. Relationships are essential to the long-term survival of a business and encourage long-term links. In order to engage in relationship marketing, different types of tactics can be used including behavioural advertising based on data analytics. This enables the identification of specific consumer segments that are then targeted more precisely through marketing campaigns. This is useful in technology marketing, which involves planning activities around satisfying organisational objectives. All forms of technology marketing emphasise value creation due to the interaction between buyer and seller being an important component of any marketing effort particularly that involving innovation.

Cyber entrepreneurship

Entrepreneurial activity should be encouraged as it is an engine of growth and indicator of economic competitiveness. Cyber entrepreneurship is a contemporary phenomenon that has gained popularity due to the emphasis on information technology communications. There is no universal definition of cyber entrepreneurship due to the variety of contexts and environments in which it can occur. Tajvidi and Tajvidi (in press: 4) define cyber entrepreneurship as "a internet-based business practice in which entrepreneurs attempt to establish their companies via an internet platform". New business ventures provide many benefits to an economy including through creating job opportunities and tax revenues. Individuals are motivated due to the need for financial gain or to remain productive. Technological advancements have led to societal changes and economic shifts. This has led to the new economy being referred to as the knowledge, online or digital economy (Tajvidi & Tajvidi, in press). The new economy is based on the need for economic and social systems to be based on technological innovation. This has led to increased customer interaction in online communities through reviews and the sharing of information. As a result, firms have had to focus more on social media as a marketing tool and way to keep engaged with customers. Social media enables firms and customers to interact in a more direct and frequent manner. This has led to customers sharing their opinions and expressing their needs. Cyber entrepreneurship provides a way for new ideas to emerge in the online environment. This new type of entrepreneurship is becoming popular due to the need to integrate digital business activities into the global economic environment.

Entrepreneurship can be broadly defined as turning innovative ideas into business ventures. This means that entrepreneurship involves some form of uncertainty in terms of outcome and risk. Entrepreneurs are a key input in the production process of the global economy. This means that entrepreneurs equilibrate supply and demand by focusing on market opportunities. Cyber entrepreneurship is a leadership style as it involves an individual pursuing an idea. This requires some level of determination and perseverance. Moreover, cyber entrepreneurs emphasise the need for online business ventures that can achieve profitable business growth.

Businesses are increasingly focusing on how to create innovative ideas in the digital economy. This means that the online environment is fostering business growth through identifying online information technology projects. Cyber entrepreneurship occurs through the exchange of data in an electronic network. This makes it important to utilise information technology for business transactions. Cyber entrepreneurs rely on technology for their business activities. This is different from traditional entrepreneurship that did not necessarily utilise cyberspace. However, existing businesses can become cyber entrepreneurs by incorporating cyberspace for extensions to their business activities.

Cyber entrepreneurship can range from low to high levels of digital technology innovation. In a low-digital technology context, the business idea is a complement, addition or supplement to existing activities. This means its introduction to the marketplace normally comes at a slower and more progressive pace. Moderate forms of cyber entrepreneurship go a step further by emphasising digital products or services. Increasingly this is becoming the norm as more businesses integrate digital components into their business activities. High levels of digital technology involve entirely new business ventures based on digital technology. This means that the business operates entirely through the digital environment.

Cyber entrepreneurs need to have knowledge of information technology. This means developing a digital business can be more complex than a traditional business but it can be easier and faster to start a digital business. This is due to the low cost of market entry and the less time-consuming process. To foster cyber entrepreneurship, knowledge needs to be exchanged in order to create value. This process can be accelerated by utilising digital collaborative tools that make the sharing of information easier. Increasingly online communities are being utilised as a source of information and knowledge. This provides a platform for cyber entrepreneurs to access information about new ideas.

Conclusion

This chapter has discussed the role of technology entrepreneurship in Indonesia. Due to the growth in the digital and knowledge economy, technology-based ventures are being prioritised in the Indonesian economy. The way in which unicorns such as Go-Jek have revolutionised the Indonesian economy were stated. This led to an examination on technology innovation and cyber entrepreneurship. In the future, it is expected that there will be further emphasis on technology innovation in Indonesia.

References

Ameen, N., Hosany, S., & Tarhini, A. (in press). Consumer interaction with cutting-edge technologies: Implications for future research. *Computers in Human Behaviour*.

Apostolopoulos, N., Ratten, V., Stavroyiannis, S., Makris, I., Apostolopoulos, S., & Liargovas, P. (2020). Rural health enterprises in the EU context: A systematic literature review and research agenda. *Journal of Enterprising Communities: People and Places in the Global Economy*, 14(4), 563–582.

Berry, L. L. (1983). Relationship marketing. *Emerging Perspectives on Services Marketing*, 66(3), 33–47.

Chesbrough, H. (2003). The logic of open innovation: Managing intellectual property. *California Management Review*, 45(3), 33–58.

Constantinides, P., Henfridsson, O., & Parker, G. (2018). Platforms and infrastructures in the digital age. *Information Systems Research*, 29, 381–400.

Feranita, F., Kotlar, J., & De Massis, A. (2017). Collaborative innovation in family firms: Past research, current debates and agenda for future research. *Journal of Family Business Strategy*, 8(3), 137–156.

Grönroos, C. (2006). Adopting a service logic for marketing. *Marketing Theory*, 6(3), 317–333.

Heiskala, R. (2007). Social innovations: Structural and power perspectives. *Social Innovations, Institutional Change and Economic Performance*, 52–79.

Huarng, K., & Yu, T. (in press). Complexity theory of entrepreneur characteristics. *International Entrepreneurship and Management Journal*.

Kahn, K. B. (2018). Understanding innovation. *Business Horizons*, 61(3), 453–460.

Park, H., Kim, S., Jeong, Y., & Minshall, T. (2021). Customer entrepreneurship on digital platforms: Challenges and solutions for platform business models. *Creativity and Innovation Management, 30*, 96–115.

Ratten, V. (2020a). Coronavirus (Covid-19) and entrepreneurship: Changing life and work landscape. *Journal of Small Business & Entrepreneurship, 32*(5), 503–516.

Ratten, V. (2020b). Coronavirus and international business: An entrepreneurial ecosystem perspective. *Thunderbird International Business Review, 62*(5), 629–634.

Rheingold, H. (1993). *The virtual community: Homesteading on the electronic frontier.* Cambridge, MA: Addison Wesley.

Shaw, E. H. (2012). Marketing strategy: From the origin of the concept to the development of a conceptual framework. *Journal of Historical Research in Marketing, 4,* 30–55.

Sprong, N., Driessen, P., Hillebrand, B., & Molner, S. (in press). Market innovation: A literature review and new research directions. *Journal of Business Research.*

Tajvidi, R., & Tajvidi, M. (in press). The growth of cyber entrepreneurship in the food industry: Virtual community engagement in the Covid-19 era. *British Food Journal.*

7 Cross-sectional study (period 2013–2016) of the factors that identify entrepreneurship in Indonesia

Mercedes Barrachina Fernández, Maria del Carmen Garcia Centeno and Carmen Calderón Patier

Introduction

Entrepreneurship is of great importance in the global economy and is a hot topic for interested public decision-makers due to its growing importance in economic activity (Thurik, 2014). It is important to highlight that the relevance of entrepreneurial business activity has quickened in recent decades, and the approach to the economy has shifted from an "administered" approach to an "entrepreneurial" focus according to different researchers (Audretsch & Thurik, 2001). Indonesia is a developing country characterised by stable economic growth and with an enriching socio-cultural diversity. The entrepreneurs are a fundamental part of the economy and support the stabilisation of the country (Ratten, 2014). Indonesia is the largest archipelago in the world, and it is composed of 5 major islands and 30 smaller ones. In total, there are around 17,500 islands, and it is estimated that one-third of them are inhabited (Adisoemarto, 2019). Statistics Indonesia (2021) has reported that the country's population has reached 270.20 million in September 2020. According to data provided by the Indonesian Ministry of Cooperatives and Small and medium-sized enterprises (SMEs), in 2018, only 3.1% of the population were entrepreneurs.

Indonesia is a republic with its capital in the city of Jakarta. Other important cities of the country, especially with a high influence in the country's economy, are Bogor, Depok, Tangerang, Bekasi and Bali. The country is rich in natural resources such as oil, natural gas, coal, tin, copper or gold and, because of them, it can be considered as one of the richest countries in the world. To understand Indonesia main figures (OECD, 2018; IMF, 2020), it is key to mention that Indonesia had an unemployment rate of 8% in 2020, the inflation rate in 2019 was 2.8%, the gross domestic product (GDP) per capita in 2020 was around 4000 dollars and almost 50% of the people is dependent on the service sector. Moreover, it is important to highlight that less than 0.1% of the GDP is invested on Research and Development (R&D) (in average, the Organisation for Economic Co-operation and Development (OECD) countries invest 2.3% of the GDP). Indonesia is a very diverse country with six official religions (Statistics

DOI: 10.4324/9781003187769-7

Indonesia, 2021): Islam (which is the religion of around 87% of the population), Protestantism (7.6% of the population), Catholicism (around 3% of the population), Hinduism (including 1.75% of the population), Buddhism (nearly 0.8% of the population) and finally Confucianism (with around 0.03% of the population). According to Arsana and Alibhai (2016), more than 90% of the companies in Indonesia are Micro, Small & Medium Enterprises (MSME), and more than 60% of the micro enterprises are led by women.

The Indonesian government has tried to encourage individuals to become entrepreneurs. The Industry Minister declared in 2018 that Indonesia needed 4 million new entrepreneurs to help with increasing the economic growth rate. Therefore, the Indonesian State Minister for Cooperatives and SMEs has performed different activities with the purpose of encouraging people to become entrepreneurs and accelerate the foundation of companies. The main objective of those activities and resources is to provide tools for the businesses to be independent, strong, competitive, self-developing and be a strategic point in the job creation process.

The main goal of this study is to evaluate the characteristics of entrepreneurship in Indonesia. The chapter is organised as follows. First, a literature review supporting the research is provided. Then, the research methodology and data collection have been highlighted along with the main results of this study, together with the discussion. Finally, conclusions, as well as limitations and future lines of research have been proposed.

Literature review

Small and medium-sized companies are key in projecting inclusive and sustainable growth, also considering factors such as social cohesion. More specifically, in OECD countries, these types of companies, also known as SMEs, represent 99% of companies, 60% of employment, and are the main drivers in some cities and regions (OECD, 2019a). There are different studies in the literature evaluating the effect of the policies regarding entrepreneurship (Castaño, Méndez, & Galindo, 2016). However, Raafaldini, Simatupang and Larso (2015) mentioned that entrepreneurship policy in entrepreneurship research has not been widely researched. This study highlights that, at the micro company level, the programs are very focused on individuals, with the purpose of increasing the number of startups businesses and also the number of entrepreneurs. Those programs are usually focused on motivation, technical skills, marketing training, management training and financial skill. However, at the macro company level, different programs have been implemented, and the focus of those programs was venture capital, entrepreneurship education and infrastructure. In recent years, the interest in women entrepreneurship has increased in popularity due to the contribution women entrepreneurship makes in the rural environment, incrementing local capabilities and increasing rural economic growth (Tambunan, 2007). Education is an important fact for entrepreneurship and according to OECD (2019b), around 90% of the young men in Indonesia are employed no matter the level of education, however, for young women, the situation is different as their employment rate is 30% higher having a tertiary education level (compared with the women only having a secondary education level).

In the literature, different public databases have been identified that focus on entrepreneurship activity. One of the main ones is the Global Entrepreneurship Monitor (GEM) database, which is the world's most important observatory on entrepreneurship. It started in 1999 and since then, it measures the entrepreneurial dynamics in more than 100 countries, thanks to a common methodology, with which it evaluates characteristics, attitudes or motivations (Asociación RED GEM España, 2019).

The mentioned database was created in September 1997 as a joint research initiative between two exceptional institutions: Babson College (United States) and London Business School (United Kingdom). The main purpose of this project was to put efforts in the entrepreneurship area and create a database with valid information to evaluate the relationship between the entrepreneurship and the economic growth. Initially, the GEM focused on the G7 countries (Canada, France, Germany, Italy, Japan, the United Kingdom and the United States) and additionally three more countries were added, due to the origin of the selected academics (Denmark, Finland and Israel) (Reynolds, 1999).

There are three characteristics that uniquely identify this database worldwide. First, there is no other similar data source with valid information about entrepreneurship with so many countries as GEM. Second, information about any type of entrepreneurship can be found in the created database. Third, all the information gathered is very focused on the initial phases of the entrepreneurship process, which is also known as "nascent entrepreneurship".

The GEM provides a strong framework in which national governments can develop a set of effective policies to improve entrepreneurship. The sources of information that feed the GEM observatory (Bergmann, Mueller, & Schrettle, 2014; Asociación RED GEM España, 2019) are the following:

1 APS: Survey of the adult population. This survey is carried out on more than 2,000 adult individuals (18–64 years) from the country analysed and mainly analyses the business aspirations of the country's population. It takes place between April and July in all participating nations and regions. NES: National Survey of Experts. This survey is carried out by a group of experts, at least 36 business and academic experts from the country analysed, and focuses on analysing the country's institutional factors. Each participating country or region selects a representative sample of experts in different fields: financing, government policies, political programs, education, R&D transfer, opening of the internal market and social regulations. These experts are interviewed between the months of March and July through a questionnaire designed by GEM.
2 Secondary sources: Every year the GEM project collects information, from July to September, from different sources that provide information

on fundamental economic variables: economic development, demography, labour market, innovation and competitiveness.

The two mentioned surveys are subjected to rigorous quality controls in relation to their translation and field work in order to guarantee that the responses obtained in all the participating countries are comparable.

Multiple articles have been found in the literature that analyse different aspects of entrepreneurship based on the GEM database. According to the study performed by Faghih, Bonyadi and Sarreshtchdari (2019), they proposed three new indices with the aim of investigating the attitude and capacity of communications, proposing a non-linear regression approach and delving into the relationship between these indices. In addition, it develops a ranking list of countries, showing that the entrepreneurial attitude dispersion index can improve the economic categorisation of countries.

In the literature, there are different types of studies related to female entrepreneurship. For example, there are studies on the classification of specific typologies (Bruni, Gherardi, & Poggio, 2004), which identify the different profiles (aimless, success-oriented, strongly success-oriented, dualist, return workers, traditionalists, radicals) for women entrepreneurs. Others focus the analysis on evaluating the relationship between female entrepreneurship and social and demographic conditions (Tominc & Rebernik, 2004; O'Gorman & Terjesen, 2006; Verheul, Van Stel, & Thurik, 2006; Noguera, Alvarez, & Urbano, 2013; Ćirec & Močnik, 2015). Other articles found are based on the characteristics of female entrepreneurship due to their success or failure in entrepreneurial activity (Justo, DeTienne, & Sieger, 2015) or focused on finding the differences between the entrepreneurial activity of men and women (Crespo, 2017). There are other articles that focus on showing the relationship between female entrepreneurship and different variables, for example, with the Better Life Index (Ribes-Giner, Moya-Clemente, Cervelló-Royo, & Perello-Marin, 2019) or the relationship between female entrepreneurship and the Country Risk Score and the Glass Ceiling Index (Ribes-Giner, Moya-Clemente, Cervelló-Royo, & Perello-Marin, 2018).

There are various studies related to the factors that affect entrepreneurship in different countries of the world, for example, Iran (Mohammadi, 2018), Romania (Dumitru, 2018) and Italy (Matricano & Sorrentino, 2018). There are authors (Chaganti, 1986; Brush, 1992) who have centred their attention on management aspects related to the phase the startup is in, reaching very interesting results, for example, that female entrepreneurs manage their companies in a more flexible way than men, women tend to avoid long-term decisions, their leadership style focuses on involving and motivating employees and not evaluating results only based on income. However, there are also studies that focus on analysing the reasons why entrepreneurs leave their businesses (Justo & Detienne, 2015). Other articles analyse the most notable differences between male and female entrepreneurship, for example, identifying that businesses created by women tend to be smaller and grow less than those with men as owners (Du Rietz & Henrekson,

2000). Specifically for Indonesia, Anggadwita, Luturlean, Ramadani and Ratten (2017) focused on exploring the socio-cultural environment on the entrepreneurial behaviour considering the involvement of women in the entrepreneurial process in Indonesia.

According to the data provided annually by the GEM database (GEM, 2018), and considering the most updated information, Indonesia has a Total early-stage Entrepreneurial Activity (TEA) of 14.09 (as average), a higher value than Australia (10.52) but lower than Thailand (19.68), for example. According to the literature, one of the most relevant problems in Indonesian workers is related to the education of the population. Only 9% of the employees are considering high skilled resources and this could be an issue when innovating.

Data and methodology

This work aims to analyse the effect of different variables (social, perceptual, economic) on female entrepreneurial activity in the period 2013–2016 in Indonesia. Data from the GEM will be used for the years 2013–2016 at the individual level for Indonesia. Table 7.1 shows the variables that have been considered in this work:

The analysis was performed with the open-source Anaconda, for working with Python to implement the method selected. The analysis of the data was initiated with a review of the available data, and an initial pre-processing was executed for cleaning the data. The analysis used a logistic regression model since, the

Table 7.1 Description of variables

Variable	Description	Source
gender	Gender: This variable will be filtered to match the female gender (value 1)	GEM Database
age	Age of the respondent	GEM Database
hhsize	Number of members in household	GEM Database
gemeduc	Education level: 1 if secondary or higher education	GEM Database
gemhhinc	Respondent income: 1 if it is in the highest 33rd percentile	GEM Database
fearfail	1 if the respondent is afraid of failure	GEM Database
suskill	1 if the respondent has confidence in his/her entrepreneurial skill	GEM Database
knowent	1 if the respondent personally knows someone who started a firm in the past two years	GEM Database
opport	1 if the respondent perceives good opportunities to start a business	GEM Database
nbgood	1 if starting a business is a desirable career choice	GEM Database
nbmedia	1 if the respondent often see stories in the public media about successful new business	GEM Database
nbstatus	1 if the respondent considers that entrepreneurs have a high level of status and respect	GEM Database
busang	1 if the respondent has personally acted as a business angel in the past 3 years	GEM Database

dependent variable takes value 1 if it is decided to launch a new business and 0 in the opposite case. Thus, with the estimated model, it will be analysed what factors of the proposed ones affect the decision to act as an entrepreneur in Indonesia. The total number of registers evaluated sums up 19.120, and, after cleaning the data, it decreased to 18.518 registers.

The hypothesis formulated in this analysis are listed later:

1 The age has a negative influence on the decision of becoming an entrepreneur in Indonesia.
2 Having a high level of education has a positive influence when deciding to become an entrepreneur in Indonesia.
3 The higher the salary of the individual the higher the propensity to become an entrepreneur in Indonesia.
4 The fear to fail influences negatively in the creation of a business in Indonesia.
5 Individuals with confidence in their abilities are more likely to act as entrepreneurs in Indonesia.
6 Having a strong entrepreneur network is a positive factor when deciding to start a business in Indonesia.
7 Perceiving good opportunities in the living area affects positively in the decision of becoming an entrepreneur in Indonesia.
8 A positive perception of entrepreneurship as a career path influences positively in the decision of becoming an entrepreneur in Indonesia.
9 Having a high level of respect for founders of businesses has a positive impact in the decision of becoming an entrepreneur in Indonesia.
10 Being used to display business successful stories in the media affects positively in the decision of becoming an entrepreneur in Indonesia.
11 Being an informal investor has a positive influence in the decision of becoming an entrepreneur.
12 Being a woman affects negatively in the decision of founding a business in Indonesia.
13 The smaller the size of the household, the higher the probability to become an entrepreneur in Indonesia.

Results

This analysis was performed using the "liblinear" library in Python, which is the one containing the logistic regression methods. The main results after the execution of the logistic regression model are displayed in Table 7.2.

Additionally, it is relevant to identify that in terms of Pseudo-R^2, the values obtained in the period analysed is 6.4%, in line with the value obtained in this type of model in other similar works.

First, it is possible to conclude that for the analysed period, age (variable *age*) has a negative and significant influence on entrepreneurship in Indonesia, which implies that the older the individual, the less likely to become entrepreneur, regardless of the economic situation of the country, confirming hypothesis 1 formulated.

Table 7.2 Results obtained from the logistic regression

Variable	Coefficient	St. deviation	p-value
age	−0.0290	0.0015	0.0000
gemeduc	−0.3563	0.0404	0.0000
gemhhinc	0.1312	0.0446	0.0033
fearfail	−0.5055	0.0405	0.0000
suskill	0.8022	0.0501	0.0000
knowent	0.3809	0.0478	0.0000
opport	0.5965	0.0435	0.0000
nbgoodc	−0.1101	0.0450	0.0144
nbstatus	−0.0486	0.0483	0.3140
nbmedia	−0.0748	0.0476	0.1162
busang	0.4879	0.0869	0.0000
gender	−0.3720	0.0345	0.0000
hhsize	−0.17074	0.0122	0.0000

Regarding the level of education (*gemeduc* variable), the variable related to the level of education is significant and negative which implies that the higher the level of education the lower propensity to become an entrepreneur in Indonesia, rejecting hypothesis 2.

The salary, represented with the *gemhhinc* variable, analyses the effect of the respondent's salary on their decision to act as an entrepreneur. The *gemhhinc* variable takes the value 1, in case the respondent has a salary in the 33rd highest percentile. For Indonesia, this variable is significant and with a positive effect confirming hypothesis 3.

Related to the fear of failure (*fearfail*), it is a significant variable with a negative effect in the decision of becoming an entrepreneur, confirming hypothesis 4.

Confidence in the own abilities, represented with variable *suskill*, affects significantly and positively in the decision of becoming an entrepreneur in Indonesia, confirming hypothesis 5.

Having a strong network composed of other entrepreneurs is a significant and positive variable when deciding to found a business, corroborating hypothesis 6.

The perception of good opportunities to start a business (*opport*) is obtained to influence positively to the decision of creating a company, supporting hypothesis 7.

When deciding to start a business, an important consideration is the career option, as it is an important step in someone's professional career. In Indonesia, contrary to what could be assumed, considering that entrepreneurship is a good career option (*nbgoodc*), negatively affects the probability of becoming an entrepreneur, rejecting hypothesis 8.

The experience acting in other businesses, as an informal investor (*busang*), is a positive fact when deciding to become an entrepreneur in Indonesia, confirming hypothesis 11.

In Indonesia, being a woman negatively influences the decision of becoming an entrepreneur (*gender*), supporting hypothesis 12.

Finally, related to the size of the household (*hhsize*), the higher the number of members in the house, the lower probability to become an entrepreneur, confirming hypothesis 13.

Evaluating the values of the coefficients influencing in the decision of becoming an entrepreneur, the highest values are assigned to the confidence (*suskill*), opportunities perception (*opport*) and having acted as an informal investor or business angel (*busang*).

Discussion

The main objective is to determine what are the factors that have contributed or not in entrepreneurship in Indonesia according to the economic situation, analysed between 2013 and 2016. In this work, the importance of entrepreneurship has been exposed and its importance in the economy as well as the entrepreneurship main facts in Indonesia. According to the model utilised, it is concluded that the following variables are significant but with a negative influence in the decision of becoming an entrepreneur in Indonesia: age (*age*), level of education (*gemeduc*), fear of failure (*fearfail*), considering entrepreneurship a good career option (*nbgoodc*), being a woman (*gender*) and the household size (*hhsize*). The results obtained are in line with other studies performed using similar variable finding that the fear to failure is having a negative impact when considering founding a business (Wyrwich, Stuetzer, & Sternberg, 2016). In the literature, the fact of being a woman has also been studied, and, in other areas, such as in Europe having similar results (Minniti, 2009; O'Gorman & Terjesen, 2006). Therefore, this result is interesting to show the policymakers the areas in which the entrepreneurship level could be improved, and, consequently, design and implement measurements that could support and foster female entrepreneurship.

The age of an individual is another factor that has been widely studied in the literature, concluding that it has a negative impact on becoming an entrepreneur (Wennekers, 2010; O'Gorman & Terjesen, 2006). In the same line, this information should be utilised to implement policies to help not only young entrepreneurs but also senior-level entrepreneurs as they have, potentially, a stronger background and experience, and this practice could be useful when founding a business.

However, the significant variables that affect positively to the decision of creating a business are: having a good salary (*gemhhinc*), having confidence in the own abilities (*suskill*), having a strong entrepreneur network (*knowent*) and perceive opportunities to start a business in the living area (*opport*) and having experience as a business angel (*busang*). Now, there is an increasing number of programs, dedicated to connecting entrepreneurs and professionals. One of the most important factors when deciding to create a new business in Indonesia is the network contacts and their entrepreneur experiences. This could be used as a justification for increasing the connections of the entrepreneurship networks by organising national or regional events for associating and networking with other entrepreneurs in the same area. The programs for providing information of how to create a business with basic information about financial resources, marketing strategies and digital training are also very useful to build trust on the own's abilities.

Conclusions

The main aim of this research was to identify the factors that characterise the entrepreneurship in Indonesia, considering different types of variables, so that policies can be articulated based on the entrepreneurship purposes. In this work, the importance of entrepreneurship in the economy has been exposed, which makes it extremely useful to know how it will evolve depending on the different decisions made in other fields, especially to promote entrepreneurship in different sectors, executing different economic and social policies. This analysis contributes to the literature by extending the knowledge related to the factors that influence entrepreneurship in Indonesia. This information could be interesting for policymakers to design policies to foster entrepreneurship between the different population groups.

There are several limitations to the results of this study. This analysis is subject to the limitations found during the execution, mainly related with the data available to be evaluated, as only information in the period 2013–2016 was feasible in the GEM Database. Even though the initial idea was to consider the last 20 years, the data from the GEM databases were not available for that period. Based on the results obtained and considering that the topic of entrepreneurship is booming due to its relationship with economic growth, for future research, it would be interesting to extend this analysis for specific groups of entrepreneurs. A possible extension of this work would consist of evaluating the differences between female and male entrepreneurs in Indonesia or to identify the factors that influence in the decision of becoming an angel investor in Indonesia. Another interesting research direction could be based on the different types of entrepreneurs identified in Indonesia, with the main purpose of identifying the main factors affecting young entrepreneurs and senior-level entrepreneurs. Another potential future study could be focused on comparing the entrepreneur's factors in Indonesia with the factors in other countries of the region with data available (e.g. Australia, New Zealand or China).

References

Adisoemarto, S. (2019). Small islands: Protect or neglect? An Indonesian case. *International Journal of Island Affairs*, *13*(1), 89–94.

Anggadwita, G., Luturlean, B. S., Ramadani, V., & Ratten, V. (2017). Socio-cultural environments and emerging economy entrepreneurship: Women entrepreneurs in Indonesia. *Journal of Entrepreneurship in Emerging Economies*, *9*(1), 85–96.

Arsana, I. G. P., & Alibhai, S. (2016). *Women entrepreneurs in Indonesia: A pathway to increasing shared prosperity (English)*. Washington, DC: World Bank Group.

Asociación RED GEM España. (2019). *Informe global entrepreneurship (GEM) España 2018–2019*. Barcelona: University of Barcelona.

Audretsch, D., & Thurik, A. R. (2001). Capitalism and democracy in the 21st century: From the managed to the entrepreneurial economy. *Journal of Evolutionary Economics, 10*, 17–34. Springer.

Bergmann, H., Mueller, S., & Schrettle, T. (2014). The use of global entrepreneurship monitor data in academic research: A critical inventory and future potentials. *International Journal of Entrepreneurial Venturing, 6*(3), 242–260.

Bruni, A., Gherardi, S., & Poggio, B. (2004). Entrepreneur – Reality, gender and the study of women entrepreneurs. *Journal of Organizational Change Management, 17*(3), 256–268.

Brush, C. (1992). Research on women business owners: Past trends, a new perspective and future directions. *Entrepreneurship Theory and Practice, 16*(4), 5–30.

Castaño, M. S., Méndez, M. T., & Galindo, M. A. (2016). The effect of public policies on entrepreneurial activity and economic growth. *Journal of Business Research, 69*(11), 5280–5285.

Chaganti, R. (1986). Management in women-owned enterprises. *Journal of Small Business Management, 24*(4), 18–29.

Ćirec, K., & Močnik, D. (2015). Gender-based determinants of innovative activity in Southeast European established entrepreneurs. In V. Ramadani, S. Gërguri-Rashiti, & A. Fayolle (Eds.), *Female entrepreneurship in transition economies*. London, UK: Palgrave Macmillan.

Crespo, N. (2017). Cross-cultural differences in the entrepreneurial activity of men and women: A fuzzy-set approach. *Gender in Management, 32*(4), 281–299.

Dumitru, I. (2018). Drivers of entrepreneurial intentions of Romania. *Romanian Journal of Economic Forecasting, 21*(1), 1.

Du Rietz, A., & Henrekson, M. (2000). Testing the female underperformance hypothesis. *Small Business Economics, 14*(1), 1–10.

Faghih, N., Bonyadi, E., & Sarreshtehdari, L. (2019). Global entrepreneurship capacity and entrepreneurial attitude indexing based on the Global Entrepreneurship Monitor (GEM) Dataset. In *Globalization and development*. London: Global Entrepreneurship Monitor consortium.

GEM. (2018). Retrieved on 10th May 2021, from www.gemconsortium.org/economy-profiles/indonesia-2.

IMF. (2020). *International Monetary Fund: World economic outlook database*. Retrieved on 10th May 2021, from www.imf.org/en/Publications/SPROLLs/world-economic-outlook-databases#sort=%40imfdate%20descending.

Justo, R., DeTienne, D. R., & Sieger, P. (2015). Failure or voluntary exit? Reassessing the female underperformance hypothesis. *Journal of Business Venturing, 30*(6), 775–792.

Matricano, D., & Sorrentino, M. (2018). Gender equalities in entrepreneurship: How close, or far, have we come in Italy? *International Journal of Business and Management, 13*(3), 75–87.

Minniti, M. (2009). Gender issues in entrepreneurship. *Foundations and Trends in Entrepreneurship, 5*, 497–621.

Mohammadi, M. (2018). Determinants of female entrepreneurship in Iran: An institutional approach. *Economic Annals, 63*(216), 111–129.

Noguera, M., Alvarez, C., & Urbano, D. (2013). Socio-cultural factors and female entrepreneurship. *International Entrepreneurship and Management Journal, 9*(2), 183–197.

OECD. (2018). Retrieved on 10th May 2021, from www.oecd.org/about/secretary-general/launch-of-oecd-review-of-sme-and-entrepreneurship-policy-in-indonesia-october-2018.htm.

OECD. (2019a). *SME and entrepreneurship outlook 2019*. Retrieved on 10th May 2021, from https://www.oecd.org/industry/oecd-sme-and-entrepreneurship-outlook-2019-34907e9c-en.htm.

OECD. (2019b). Retrieved on 10th May 2021, from www.oecd.org/education/education-at-a-glance/EAG2019_CN_IDN.pdf.

O'Gorman, C., & Terjesen, S. (2006). Financing the Celtic Tigress: Venture financing and informal investment in Ireland. *Venture Capital*, 8(1), 69–88.

Raafaldini, I., Simatupang, T., & Larso, D. (2015). Mapping on entrepreneurship policy in Indonesia. *Procedia – Social and Behavioral Sciences*, 169, 346–353.

Ratten, V. (2014). Encouraging collaborative entrepreneurship in developing countries: The current challenges and a research agenda. *Journal of Entrepreneurship in Emerging Economies*, 6(3), 298–308.

Reynolds, P. (1999). *Global Entrepreneurship Monitor: 1999 Executive report*. Babson: Babson College.

Ribes-Giner, G., Moya-Clemente, I., Cervelló-Royo, R., & Perello-Marin, M. R. (2018). Domestic economic and social conditions empowering female entrepreneurship. *Journal of Business Research*, 89, 182–189.

Ribes-Giner, G., Moya-Clemente, I., Cervelló-Royo, R., & Perello-Marin, M. R. (2019). Wellbeing indicators affecting female entrepreneurship in OECD countries. *Quality & Quantity: International Journal of Methodology*, 53(2), 915–933.

Statistics Indonesia. (2021). Retrieved on 1st March 2021, from www.bps.go.id.

Tambunan, T. (2007). Entrepreneurship development: SMES in Indonesia. *Journal of Developmental Entrepreneurship*, 12(1), 95–118.

Thurik, R. (2014). Entrepreneurship and the business cycle. *IZA World of Labour 2014*, 90. Retrieved on 10th May 2021, from doi:10.15185/izawol.90

Tominc, P., & Rebernik, M. (2004). The scarcity of female entrepreneurship. *Journal for General Social Issues*, 13(4), 779–802.

Verheul, I., Van Stel, A., & Thurik, R. (2006). Explaining female and male entrepreneurship at the country level. *Entrepreneurship & Regional Development*, 18(2), 151–183.

Wennekers, S., Van Stel, A., Carree, M., & Thurik, R. (2010). *The relationship between entrepreneurship and economic development: Is it U-Shaped?* New York: Now Publishers Inc.

Wyrwich, M., Stuetzer, M., & Sternberg, R. (2016). Entrepreneurial role models, fear of failure, and institutional approval of entrepreneurship: A tale of two regions. *Small Business Economics*, 46(3), 467–492.

8 Rural entrepreneurship and social innovation in Indonesia

Vanessa Ratten

Introduction

Increasingly entrepreneurship research is emphasising the role of context. This means that greater care is taken in understanding the role of rural areas in entrepreneurial activity. Rural entrepreneurship needs to be understood in terms of its historical and social role in business activity. The rural context influences the range of business activities that are available in a region. Therefore, rural areas can provide benefits as well as disadvantages for entrepreneurs. In order for rural entrepreneurs to survive and prosper, they need to be innovative. Fitz-Koch, Norqvist, Carter and Hunter (2018: 130) state that "agriculture is amongst the world's largest sectors, employing over one billion people and accounting for 3% of global GDP". This means that it is an important context from which to study entrepreneurial behaviour. Moreover, there has been increased interaction of agri-business activities into other sectors of the economy including through tourism and education.

Although the practical importance of rural areas in the global economy is evident, mainstream entrepreneurship research has tended to neglect the agricultural industry due to an emphasis on technology contexts. This is worrying as there are many different ways the agricultural sector is entrepreneurial including through the startup of new businesses and integration of technology innovation into business activities. In addition, there has been an abundance of research on the agricultural industry in the economics and sociology fields but less in an entrepreneurship context. This has meant most of the existing studies on agricultural entrepreneurship have their roots in other fields.

Stathopoulou, Psaltopoulos and Skuras (2004: 404) state that "rurality defines a territorially specific entrepreneurial milieu with distinct physical, social and economic characteristics". This means that rural areas are characterised by the landscape and environmental context that differentiates them from urban areas. The natural resources found in a rural area often provides an opportunity for specific types of entrepreneurship to occur, namely around farming and agriculture. However, there can be a difference amongst rural areas based on their geographic proximity to other areas. This means that there are more remote rural areas that are difficult to enter because of the terrain. Often more remote rural areas are less

DOI: 10.4324/9781003187769-8

populated and have a high dependence on farming. This results in infrastructural inadequacies that can make it hard to transform into more value-added activities.

The under-development in rural areas makes it ripe for entrepreneurs. Research into rural entrepreneurship is still sparse and lacks the substantial number of publications prevalent in other entrepreneurship research fields. This means research into the effects and dynamics of rural entrepreneurship can shed light on new entrepreneurial practices. The objective of this chapter is to present an integrated framework on rural entrepreneurship taking into account social innovations. To do this, the chapter will review and discuss the contextual issues associated with rural, agricultural and farm entrepreneurship, thereby arguing that the process of rural entrepreneurship is not very different from that found in other contexts but rather depends on environmental factors.

Agricultural entrepreneurship

Agricultural entrepreneurship is synonymous with the rural context and especially relates to farming activities. This means, in its broadest sense, agricultural entrepreneurship refers to the cultivation of rural products for economic gain. This includes crop plants or livestock products that are traded in the marketplace. Agricultural entrepreneurship is also referred to as farm or rural entrepreneurship. Whilst all forms of entrepreneurship have a spatial nature in terms of being location-specific, agricultural entrepreneurship requires a rural environment. This involves using the natural environment for farming pursuits. Agricultural activities have a positive impact on regions as they provide financial income, food security and alleviate poverty. Ataei, Karimi, Ghadermarzi and Norovzi (2020: 186) define a SME as "a business that recruits 150 or fewer people and possesses no integration with a public limited company". Small and medium-sized enterprises (SMEs) are a large component of the rural sector. They play a significant role in the use of entrepreneurship in agricultural businesses.

Remote areas including mountainous and less favoured areas are prone to economic inefficiencies. This means, unlike city and urban areas, there is often difficulties in gaining access to these regions for entrepreneurial activity. The high dependence on farming means there is a reliance on agriculture. This leads to a fragile socio-economic environment that is reliant on weather and soil terrain for farming activity (Brouder, 2012). Some rural areas are experiencing a new inflow of entrepreneurs that have relocated to these areas because of lifestyle factors. Entrepreneurs are also attracted to rural areas because of their lower cost of living and abundance of natural resources. This means that there is a prospect of a better standard of living. In addition, due to the Covid-19 crisis, more people are working from home, which means they have the ability to live in rural locations. Many individuals are unable or unwilling to leave rural areas because of their family or social connections. This means that there is a need to find non-farm activities that can support farming activities. The increased diversity in income means that there is more stability and growth in rural areas.

Rural entrepreneurs are characterised by their independent nature and risk-taking behaviour. This means that they emphasise achievement in their business dealings by pursuing opportunities (Cassel & Pashkevich, 2014). Agricultural innovation is a way to promote growth in rural areas. Innovation refers to an attempt to make an idea a business reality. This includes ideas about new products that can be put into practice (Booyens & Rogerson, 2017). In an agricultural setting, innovation can include changes in technology or ecological systems that result in increased performance gains. Innovation does not occur in a vacuum as it requires human interaction.

Farm entrepreneurship

Farmers are trying to reduce their risks by diversifying into other business activities. This means moving away from purely traditional farming activities to include other business ventures outside farms. This move is a strategic way farmers can maintain existing revenue sources whilst growing their businesses. The concept of portfolio management is a way to describe farm entrepreneurs having multiple concurrent business ventures. To exploit changes in the rural environment, farmers have focused on entrepreneurship as a way of providing business development. Entrepreneurship is generally concerned with the pursuit of innovative business opportunities. This means that it is important to understand why, when and how entrepreneurship occurs in an agricultural context. Identifying entrepreneurial opportunities in a rural context is a way to increased financial revenue and to transform existing activity.

There are a variety of different types of farm entrepreneurs from traditional growers to social farmers (De Lauwere, 2005). Traditional growers focus on specialised crops that have been popular in the marketplace for a long time. This means striving for more economies of scale in their farming activities. Social farmers try to encourage social responsibility in their products. This means emphasising community benefits of farms in terms of having an enhanced rural landscape. Farmers who have been in an area for a long time are normally characterised by financial conservatism. This usually means they have less of a growth orientation compared to newer farmers. Agricultural innovation is influenced by farm location and landscape patterns. This means farms that are rurally attractive and close to urban areas can also be tourist attractions. Rural entrepreneurship is instrumental in affecting the economic development of other sectors. This occurs by enhancing the productivity of a region and improving the quality of life in a rural area.

Historically farmers could rely on the constant demand from the marketplace for their products. This has changed due to shifting demands, new production methods and increased internationalisation of the agricultural industry. As a result, farmers now operate in a highly competitive marketplace. Moreover, in the past, there were price subsidies, tariff protection and regulatory restrictions on farming. This has changed with the shift to an open marketplace. Research on farm entrepreneurship is sparse despite the economic effects of farming. An entrepreneurial culture in farming can lead to greater efficiencies. This means that there are a number of competing strategies that farmers can implement such as increasing production or focusing on a new market. In addition, farmers can integrate forward or backward into the value chain by producing necessary equipment or selling produce. Moreover, there is pressure on farmers to move up the value chain in order to access more profitable activities. This enables them to be portfolio entrepreneurs by taking on multiple business projects at the same time. Portfolio entrepreneurship in farming is needed due to changes in consumer demands such as wanting a continuous availability of products and pesticide-free produce have influenced new farming activities. The growing power of supermarkets has changed the industry dynamics. This has resulted in demand for lower prices whilst increasing quality issues.

Farm entrepreneurs need to have five main skills: professional, management, opportunity, strategic and cooperation/networking (De Wolf, McElwee, & Schoorlemmer, 2007). Professional skills involve specific knowledge that takes time to learn (Brooker & Joppe, 2014). In the farming context, this can include production methods and technical information. Management skills involve knowledge about leadership and people management skills. This is important to farmers in terms of managing their workforce. Opportunity skills involve the ability to foresee change and act on it accordingly (Ferreira, Fernandes, & Ratten, 2017). This is useful in the changing competitive marketplace that is focused on innovation. Strategic skills mean developing and acting upon plans. This is needed in terms of thinking about the future and how farming will change. Cooperation/networking skills involve the ability to interact and form relationships with others (Hjalager, 2009). Farmers need to do this in order to build bridges with others who can then help them in their business ventures.

Farmers utilise portfolio entrepreneurship as a risk management strategy in order to reduce risks associated with one business activity. Entrepreneurs may decide to establish a new business that is concurrent with their existing businesses (Fierro, Noble, Hatem, & Balunywa, 2018). The reason for this can be due to a need to circumvent existing structures or to diversify business practices. Fierro et al. (2018: 732) define portfolio entrepreneurship as "the creation and management of multiple entrepreneurial ventures in a concurrent manner". Portfolio entrepreneurship normally is the result of changing market conditions requiring new business practices. As startups progress in the marketplace, decisions can then be made as to divest or continue with the business. Portfolio entrepreneurs can have an interest in multiple projects, thereby enabling them to diversify their business.

Entrepreneurs are increasingly owning and managing several businesses (Kahn, 2018). This is referred to as serial entrepreneurship and is defined as when an "entrepreneur successively creates and manages new entrepreneurial ventures one at a time" (Fierro et al., 2018: 732). This enables them to use their business experiences in other contexts. Serial entrepreneurship is common in the farming sector due to the need to obtain income from multiple sources. Farmers need to be entrepreneurial in order to obtain new skills. Agricultural production is one of the most important factors in rural economies. Tourism in a farm setting is referred to as agrotourism and is an example of serial entrepreneurship based on a portfolio approach (McKercher & Du Cros, 2003). Often agrotourism incorporates a social element in terms of bridging societal change with innovative activities.

Social innovation in agriculture

A broad definition of social innovation is some form of innovation that is social in terms of usage (Lee, Spanjol & Sun, 2019). This can include agrotourism innovation that has a social purpose or utilises social ideas. Individuals are motivated to be social innovators due to observing or experiencing hardship (Avelino, Dumitru, Cipolla, Kunze, & Wittmayer, 2020). This empathy makes them want to produce innovations that can solve societal problems. By responding to problems with care and compassion then the problem can be solved in a more humane way. There is much learning that goes into producing a social innovation as the emphasis is on positive change (Marques, Morgan, & Richardson, 2018). This means social innovation results from an exploration of possibilities by considering different actions and which ones might be more appropriate (Castro-Arce & Vanclay, 2020). To do this can be difficult due to decisions being made that weigh up costs with benefits. As there are always trade-offs being made when developing a social innovation, it is important to consider the likely impact of the change.

The idea of social innovation is premised on a world based on cooperation and change (Potts & Ratten, 2016). This means social rights such as equality and sustainability are encouraged. Once a social innovation has been developed, it requires its adoption by members of society (Edwards-Schachter & Wallace, 2017). Social innovation is hard to measure as it is based on perceptions. This means more readily available measures such as patents and R&D spending have been used as proxy for innovation (Stamboulis & Skayannis, 2003).

Social innovation is not a new concept as it has been in existence for some time (Batle, Orfila, & Moon, 2018). Although the way social innovation is developed in society has changed due to increased levels of globalisation and technology. In the past, innovation that had a social component was prevalent in society but assumed as a normal part of the economy (Ratten, 2011). It was used as a way to help those in need but due to the rise of technology-based innovations it was often overlooked. Social innovation as a term is so often used that its original conceptualisation in a tourism context can be forgotten (Ratten, Ferreira, & Fernandes, 2017). Initially, social innovation referred to change of a business nature but has since become ubiquitous with anything altering societal conduct. This means that social innovation is a victim of its own popularity. Social innovation involves new practices to emerge in a social context (Drucker, 1987). This enables intentional action to develop around a targeted topic.

Social innovation involves an initiative that changes a social system (Ratten, 2017). This means the existing products or processes are altered in a way that produces a social gain. Social innovation as a concept can be vague due to the way it is used in society (Neumeier, 2017). Some view it as the study of non-profit activity that is innovative in nature. Although it does not have to be non-profit based and can be profit orientated in nature. This occurs when organisations see a market opportunity to produce products that have a concurrent social purpose. Increasingly social goals are viewed by organisations as being necessary in today's global environment that emphasises social equality (Heiscala, 2007).

Typically, innovation has been considered more of a business function so the introduction of a social element to innovation acknowledges the need to think about societal consequences. When a social innovation occurs, the existing routines or beliefs are changed. This produces a broader societal impact that has flow-on effects. Social innovation is a dynamic process that requires the recognition of an opportunity then a resulting action (Pol & Ville, 2009). The ability to produce social innovations enables vulnerable populations to be considered. Social systems are complex as they are based on interaction amongst a group of entities in society. There are multiple interchangeable elements within a social system that enable procedures to occur.

Social innovation involves deriving new ideas that meet social goals (Oeij, Van der Torre, Vaas, & Dhondt, 2019). This means creatively thinking about problems occurring in society then producing innovative ideas to solve them. Social innovation results from a process of change that produces new ways of thinking. This means that social innovation is an essential part of society as it enables a focus on the collective good. Due to increased levels of inequality in society, social innovation is becoming more important. Moreover, societal issues such as global warming and poverty mean that social innovations are needed. Therefore, the advantage of social innovation is that it enables unthinkable possibilities to emerge.

Social innovation can range in design from a technologically advanced idea to a more incremental hands-on approach. Small changes that are based on interactive steps are referred to as incremental innovation. This type of innovation is important as it produces continual change. Not all forms of social innovation need to result in monumental change as slight alterations can produce good results. This means that it is important to think about social innovation as enhancing existing systems in order to produce more social gain. More substantial changes to society that occur as a result of social innovation are referred to as radical innovations. Due to the major changes that result from radical innovation, they are less common in society. This means that radical innovations are less likely to occur in society as they are uncommon, they still do occur but on a less frequent basis.

Social innovation can occur in a planned way in terms of it being considered based on a step-by-step process (Rao-Nicholson, Vorley, & Khan, 2017). This approach is widely used by social innovators who have specific ideas about what kind of help is needed. Although taking a planned approach does not always work well as sometimes serendipity plays a part in the development of an innovation. This means that, by chance, encounters or discoveries are an important component of social innovation. In addition, as many forms of social innovation require a stakeholder perspective, it is right to assume that feedback will help move an idea forward (Ziegler, 2017).

Social innovation tries to attain better outcomes for those at the periphery of society. This means replacing older practices with more equal and progressive practices. This can involve introducing new procedures that differ from the past but produce better results. To do this, collective action is needed by government, business and individuals in order to produce the change. Social innovation does not necessarily align with economic rationality as it considers social needs as being most important. Although economic and social goals do not need to be separated and can work in tandem, social innovation involves a new configuration of social practices in order to produce social change. This means answering needs of individuals who are promoted by societal conditions.

Need for social innovation in the agricultural sector

Social innovation represents an important addition to agriculture and rural entrepreneurship studies as it stresses the social nature of innovation. Whilst the term 'innovation' tends to imply a business result in the form of increased profitability or additional market share, there are some forms of innovation that have a social nature. This means the reason for their introduction into the marketplace is to solve a social problem. Due to the emphasis on a free market economy in many regions of the world, there has been decreased levels of government intervention. This has resulted in a need for social innovators to address inequalities not being solved by government policy. Social innovation thereby acts as a critical feature of any economy interested in the well-being of its citizens. Moreover, due to inequalities between developed and developing countries, social innovation acts as a way to increase living standards. The global economy emphasises innovation as a way to increase not only competitiveness but also wealth creation. This has led to innovation being seen as a solution to global problems that have not yet been solved.

Social innovation is a type of innovation that refers to improvements made to increase living standards. It is the same as traditional forms of innovation in terms of creating new products or processes but goes a step further in combining a social need. Societal impacts are being emphasised more due to the realisation that the world needs to consider issues such as sustainability in order to preserve and improve living standards. Social innovation can be considered as a driver of institutional change in terms of moving towards a more progressive society. This means focusing on humanity and the collective good rather than pure profit motives. Innovation typically has an economic motivation but it can also occur based on cultural conditions. When culture is considered part of the reason for an innovation then it is likely to be termed 'social innovation'. Innovation generally involves putting into action ideas about how to improve something for economic reasons.

The main principle of social innovation is that the collective good needs to be prioritised instead of individual gain. Mutual help in terms of cooperatives and philanthropic business models can lead to societal gain. The pace of social innovation is expected to accelerate due to the need for find solutions to global problems. Social innovations are primarily diffused through rural enterprises that have a social objective in addition to financial goals. This means that some rural enterprises are motivated by a need to help others that are less fortunate. There are more social innovations that have moved from being niche business entities to mainstream business models. This includes websites such as Wikipedia that was established with the goal of providing free information regardless of income level. The Wikipedia business model is based on volunteers providing updated entries on topics of interest. In addition, microfinance and crowdfunding finance models have risen with the increased interest globally about funding social projects. This means that due to the internet more information about social projects that need finance or help are available online.

Ideas for social innovation are generated from a number of different sources. This includes obvious needs in a community such as homelessness. Other ideas derive from less obvious sources such as racial inequality. Moulaert, Martinelli, Swyngedouw and Gonzalez (2005) suggest that the main dimensions of social innovation are meeting an unmet need, changing social relations and empowering individuals. Satisfying human needs can take a variety of different forms. Increasing the lack of access to certain services from clean drinking water to affordable internet services is becoming important.

Due to global challenges in the area of social policies, more interest in how to use innovation to solve social inequalities has emerged. Social innovation tries to achieve change for the collective good of society. This means doing good through investing in social innovation principles. Innovation means change but this change does not necessarily produce good or bad results. Social innovation is a purposeful form of change as it gives a sense of direction to innovative action. Thus, social innovation involves developing then deploying solutions to solve social problems. This means investing in solutions to social issues that can include environmental and sustainability concerns. These solutions often need the support of stakeholders who when working together for a collective goal can produce a change.

Social innovation can be evaluated in terms of achieving set outcomes. This includes activities that are part of an action plan designed to reduce distress in society. Social value refers to non-financial impacts and interventions that result in better living standards. This means that they are hard to quantify due to their social nature. Social change is a process that results in alterations in societal conduct. These changes are not necessarily desirable by all but result in the overall quality of life for most being improved.

Social innovation is a term that normally refers to change that has a positive effect on society. The emphasis on the word social can mean that it has a non-profit or inclusive nature. Social innovation plays an important role in the economy and society due to the flow-on effects it produces. This is due to it creating a capacity for action that leads to increased living or working conditions. Social innovation creates new capacities for action by focusing on societal problems. In society, there are many vexing social problems and unmet social needs. This makes it important for rural enterprises to move beyond traditional profit motives to also incorporate social responsibility metrics. This will enable rural businesses to undertake both business and social activities. The private sector plays a key role in changing entrenched social issues in society. They can do this by strategically investing in priority areas that help address key problems. To be a social innovator, companies need to utilise cross-sector partnerships that occur when business, government and other entities collaborate on a project. In order to have a good cross-sector partnership, both private and public entities need to collaborate. This will enable a clear business and social agenda to emerge that serves multiple purposes. A successful partnership will also involve partners that are committed to social change and have a long-term commitment.

Social innovators need to have an ability to engage with multiple stakeholders such as customers, competitors and regulators. This ability enables them to produce ideas that can then result in societal change. To encourage social innovation, there is a focus on creating hybrid solutions that meet business and social goals. This means encouraging rural businesses not only to have a central for-profit purpose but also to engage in social issues. Social movements in the form of beliefs and opinions have influenced the process of social innovation. Increasingly consumers are prioritising social issues such as climate change and recycling in their purchase decisions. This is then creating a flow-on effect by influencing firm behaviour.

Conclusion

This chapter has focused on the importance of the agricultural sector in Indonesia, thereby focusing on the role rural industries play in terms of growth and competitiveness. It is important that more emphasis is placed on the way farmers are entrepreneurial and contribute to Indonesia's economic development. This means discussing the role of social innovation in farming and rural entrepreneurship.

References

Ataei, P., Karimi, H., Ghadermarzi, H., & Norovzi, A. (2020). A conceptual model of entrepreneurial competencies and their impacts in rural youth's intention to launch SME. *Journal of Rural Studies, 75*, 185–195.

Avelino, F., Dumitru, A., Cipolla, C., Kunze, I., & Wittmayer, J. (2020). Translocal empowerment in transformative social innovation networks. *European Planning Studies, 28*(5), 955–977.

Batle, J., Orfila-Sintes, F., & Moon, C. J. (2018). Environmental management best practices: Towards social innovation. *International Journal of Hospitality Management, 69*, 14–20.

Booyens, I., & Rogerson, C. M. (2017). Networking and learning for tourism innovation: Evidence from the Western Cape. *Tourism Geographies, 19*(3), 340–361.

Brooker, E., & Joppe, M. (2014). Developing a tourism innovation typology: Leveraging liminal insights. *Journal of Travel Research, 53*(4), 500–508.

Brouder, P. (2012). Creative outposts: Tourism's place in rural innovation. *Tourism Planning & Development, 9*(4), 383–396.

Cassel, S. H., & Pashkevich, A. (2014). World Heritage and tourism innovation: Institutional frameworks and local adaptation. *European Planning Studies*, 22(8), 1625–1640.

Castro-Arce, K., & Vanclay, F. (2020). Transformative social innovation for sustainable rural development: An analytical framework to assist community-based initiatives. *Journal of Rural Studies*, 74, 45–54.

De Lauwere, C. C. (2005). The role of agricultural entrepreneurship in Dutch agriculture of today. *Agricultural Economics*, 33(2), 229–238.

De Wolf, P., McElwee, G., & Schoorlemmer, H. (2007). The European farm entrepreneur: A comparative perspective. *International Journal of Entrepreneurship and Small Business*, 4(6), 679–692.

Drucker, P. F. (1987). Social innovation – Management's new dimension. *Long Range Planning*, 20(6), 29–34.

Edwards-Schachter, M., & Wallace, M. L. (2017). 'Shaken, but not stirred': Sixty years of defining social innovation. *Technological Forecasting and Social Change*, 119, 64–79.

Ferreira, J. J., Fernandes, C. I., & Ratten, V. (2017). Entrepreneurship, innovation and competitiveness: What is the connection? *International Journal of Business and Globalisation*, 18(1), 73–95.

Fierro, A., Noble, A., Hatem, O., & Balunywa, W. (2018). African portfolio entrepreneurship and the creation of jobs. *Journal of Small Business and Enterprise Development*, 25(5), 730–751.

Fitz-Koch, S., Norqvist, M., Carter, S., & Hunter, E. (2018). Entrepreneurship in the agricultural sector: A literature review and future research opportunities. *Entrepreneurship Theory & Practice*, 42(10), 129–166.

Heiscala, R. (2007). Social innovations: Structural and power perspectives. In T. Hamalainen & R. Heiscala (Eds.), *Social innovations, institutional change and economic performance* (pp. 52–79). Cheltenham: Edward Elgar Publishing.

Hjalager, A. M. (2009). Cultural tourism innovation systems – The Roskilde festival. *Scandinavian Journal of Hospitality and Tourism*, 9(2–3), 266–287.

Kahn, K. (2018). Understanding innovation. *Business Horizons*, 61, 453–460.

Lee, R. P., Spanjol, J., & Sun, S. L. (2019). Social innovation in an interconnected world: Introduction to the special issue. *Journal of Product Innovation Management*, 36(6), 662–670.

Marques, P., Morgan, K., & Richardson, R. (2018). Social innovation in question: The theoretical and practical implications of a contested concept. *Environment and Planning C: Politics and Space*, 36(3), 496–512.

McKercher, B., & Du Cros, H. (2003). Testing a cultural tourism typology. *International Journal of Tourism Research*, 5, 45–58.

Moulaert, F., Martinelli, F., Swyngedouw, E., & Gonzalez, S. (2005). Towards alternative model(s) of local innovation. *Urban Studies*, 42(11), 1969–1990.

Neumeier, S. (2017). Social innovation in rural development: Identifying the key factors of success. *The Geographical Journal*, 183(1), 34–46.

Oeij, P. R., van der Torre, W., Vaas, F., & Dhondt, S. (2019). Understanding social innovation as an innovation process: Applying the innovation journey model. *Journal of Business Research*, 101, 243–254.

Pol, E., & Ville, S. (2009). Social innovation: Buzz word or enduring term? *The Journal of Socio-Economics*, 38, 878–885.

Potts, J., & Ratten, V. (2016). Sports innovation: Introduction to the special section. *Innovation, 18*(3), 233–237.

Rao-Nicholson, R., Vorley, T., & Khan, Z. (2017). Social innovation in emerging economies: A national systems of innovation based approach. *Technological Forecasting and Social Change, 121*, 228–237.

Ratten, V. (2011). Social entrepreneurship and innovation in sports. *International Journal of Social Entrepreneurship and Innovation, 1*(1), 42–54.

Ratten, V. (2017). *Entrepreneurship, innovation and smart cities.* London, UK: Routledge.

Ratten, V., Ferreira, J. J., & Fernandes, C. I. (2017). Innovation management- current trends and future directions. *International Journal of Innovation and Learning, 22*(2), 135–155.

Stamboulis, Y., & Skayannis, P. (2003). Innovation strategies and technology for experience-based tourism. *Tourism Management, 24*(1), 35–43.

Stathopoulou, S., Psaltopoulos, D., & Skuras, D. (2004). Rural entrepreneurship in Europe: A research framework and agenda. *International Journal of Entrepreneurial Behaviour & Research, 10*(6), 404–425.

Ziegler, R. (2017). Social innovation as a collaborative concept. *Innovation: The European Journal of Social Science Research, 30*(4), 388–405.

9 Indonesian entrepreneurship
Future directions

Vanessa Ratten

Introduction

Research on Indonesian entrepreneurship is under-represented in the literature despite its cultural significance and impact on economic growth. The encouraging news is that this is changing with an increased focus on the Indonesian economy in international business affairs. Therefore, it is necessary to build research on Indonesian entrepreneurship by providing a deeper understanding of entrepreneurship as experienced by those engaged in this activity. Western theories are dominant in entrepreneurship research, so new cultural and national contexts are needed in order to facilitate theoretical developments.

In the Indonesian entrepreneurship field, there is an expanding volume of interest from academic researchers, government policy and program developers, practitioners, the business community and leaders in entrepreneurship. This means that Indonesian entrepreneurship should emerge as one of the fastest growing fields in entrepreneurship studies. There is a scarcity of comparative studies on Indonesian entrepreneurship particularly studies comparing Indonesian and non-Indonesian approaches. Thus, this book is motivated by the desire to offer fresh insights into the entrepreneurship field by focusing on the Indonesian context. This will provide a voice for those interested in Indonesia and build a community of scholars around Indonesian entrepreneurship.

The phenomenon of Indonesian entrepreneurship is well presented in practice but less so in an academic sense. This is the result of the entrepreneurial environment in Indonesia rapidly evolving due to continued socio-cultural change. There is recognition in Indonesia about the need for entrepreneurship not only to increase economic growth rates but also to remedy systemic problems in society. This includes reducing inequality and poverty levels. This book has provided novel insights into a range of emerging topics in an Indonesian context. Recently, there has been a significant investment in Indonesia in entrepreneurial ecosystems, which has meant that entrepreneurship scholars are embracing a more contextualised understanding of entrepreneurship.

The amount of research on Indonesia is expected to expand in the future. The future of Indonesian-focused research is bright and full of opportunities. Indonesian entrepreneurship research can contribute to the current and future business

DOI: 10.4324/9781003187769-9

environment. The aim of this chapter is to create a dynamic and continuous platform to discuss Indonesian entrepreneurship research. This chapter reviews the existing literature on Indonesian entrepreneurship, including suggestions about the future growth of interest in this topic. Therefore, this chapter will lay the foundation for the contribution of this book to entrepreneurship literature.

Indonesia

Indonesia is a country located in Southeast Asia. It is officially called the Republic of Indonesia since gaining its independence. It is an archipelago comprised of a number of islands. Indonesia is the world's largest island country as it includes a large number of islands of various sizes. The largest island is Java, on which the capital Jakarta is located. The unifying features of Indonesia include a common language, history and economic interests. Indonesia is the only Association of Southeast Asian Nations (ASEAN) member in the G20. Indonesia is already a global player, but its position is expected to rise in the future. This is due to the young population and increasingly technological savvy culture. Indonesia is a geopolitical leader within Southeast Asia and its close proximity to other emerging economies impacts business relationships in the region. Indonesia is increasingly investing in education particularly of an entrepreneurial nature. This will further increase the entrepreneurial potential of the country. Indonesia has a democratic culture with high numbers of the overall population voting in elections. The six official religions in Indonesia include Buddhism, Catholicism, Confucianism, Hinduism, Islam and Protestantism although there are many other religions practised in the country. This is due to Indonesia being an ethnically diverse and multi-faith country.

The islands comprising Indonesia are spread through an area of land between Australia and Asia. Indonesia was granted independence from its previous Dutch rule in 1949 and is currently the largest economy in Southeast Asia with a strong growth rate. Indonesia is comprised of a number of distinct ethnic groups. In Indonesia, the saying 'tak kenal maka tak sayang' means that if we do not know each other we do not care about each other. Thus, there is an emphasis on interpersonal relationships to build connections that then lead to business ventures being produced. This means that knowing others can facilitate knowledge sharing and information dissemination. The entrepreneurship literature has focused on China and India as emerging economies whilst overlooking Indonesia. Therefore, the entrepreneurship spotlight needs to shift to focus more on Indonesia. In order to facilitate more entrepreneurship, there are structural changes still needed in Indonesia.

Entrepreneurship in Indonesia

Entrepreneurship in Indonesia is dynamic and constantly changing. The past decade has witnessed a rise in interest on entrepreneurship. The popular enthusiasm is due to increased international focus on entrepreneurship and its contribution to economic growth. Indonesian entrepreneurship builds on the existing research on emerging economy entrepreneurship but focuses on a country context, thereby making a critical contribution to the broad entrepreneurship literature. Indonesian-specific research on entrepreneurship enables researchers to incorporate cultural, historical, political and religious contexts, thereby extending and revising theories by considering the country context. Most of the entrepreneurship research is based on a North American or European perspective (Cavallo, Ghezzi, & Sanasi, in press). This means that our understanding of entrepreneurship is reliant on the cultural conditions apparent in developed countries. Whilst this is changing, there is still a substantial gap of literature focusing on emerging economy contexts like Indonesia. Given the unique cultural and economic context of Indonesia, it is timely that this book focuses specifically on Indonesian entrepreneurship.

Indonesia is amongst the world's largest and fastest growing economies. The unique nature of entrepreneurship in Indonesia offers the potential to bring new insights. The economic impact of Indonesia is expanding due to its geopolitical role and rising middle class. Indonesia has a rich cultural history that influences the way entrepreneurship is conducted. The liberalisation of market conditions in Indonesia has kick-started an ambitious emphasis on entrepreneurship. This has meant the adoption of market principles existing in other countries and improved working conditions. Indonesia represents an attractive market destination for individual investors and international firms. This is evident with recent statistics highlighting the growth of emerging markets in the global economy. For example, Cavusgil (2021: 1) states "emerging market economies accounted for only about 30 percent of world GDP in 1990, but now make up some 42 percent of world's GDP". The importance of entrepreneurship in Indonesia stems beyond the confines of a single country but extends to other countries. This means that the economies surrounding Indonesia in Southeast Asia can benefit from the entrepreneurial activity occurring in Indonesia. Moreover, the Indonesian diaspora that lives in other countries can also contribute to entrepreneurial activity. Thus, the Indonesian economy has both a direct and indirect effect on other economies. Indonesia has opened up its economy to international competition. As part of this growth, international marketing has been emphasised due to the way it can stimulate the economy.

Indonesia has much potential in terms of the opportunities and growth evident in a region. Some markets will be more conducive than other markets due to their favourable conditions. This makes it important to identify the most appropriate markets for a firm given their growth strategy. This process needs to consider timing issues in terms of the number of consumers and suitability of the market for a firm's product. Moreover, the potential of a market can be impacted by other environmental factors such as economic, political and social conditions (Jones, Ratten, Klapper, & Fayolle, 2019). This makes it useful to monitor international markets to see if conditions are changing or remaining the same.

In order to develop an entrepreneurial culture, it is important to focus on learning (Jones, Ratten, & Hayduk, 2020). This is due to entrepreneurship being fundamentally a behavioural process based on social interactions. Individuals constantly interact with others that then result in new knowledge being acquired. Based on this knowledge, business ventures are then started that fill a gap in the market.

Entrepreneurship

The amount of entrepreneurship occurring in Indonesia continues to rise. Entrepreneurs tend to have an open mindset that helps them engage in new ideas (Ratten, 2020a). This openness is evident in their mental attitude that enables them to see new opportunities in the marketplace. Entrepreneurs are also conscientious in the way they pursue new ideas. This enables them to focus on the goals that are relevant to their business ventures. Zhao, Ritchie and Echtner (2011: 1571) state that the essence of entrepreneurship is "the initiation of change through creativity or innovation that usually bears risk". This means within any type of entrepreneurship is a sense of creativity, innovation and risk. The creativity means it is a new way of looking at things that has previously not been considered. This can occur by introducing fresh insights that pave the way for future change. Innovation involves doing something in a new way, thereby altering existing practices (Mendoza-Silva, in press). Risk means there is some uncertainty as to what the action will produce. This includes unknown outcomes in terms of market readiness and adoption levels. Entrepreneurs discover opportunities before others in the marketplace. To detect and act upon opportunities takes time and skills. Entrepreneurs do this by seeing value in market gaps and then seizing the opportunity (Ratten, 2020b).

Entrepreneurs coordinate resources by taking initiative to turn ideas into a business reality. Entrepreneurs are normally individuals who start a business although this requirement has evolved to include those involved in the process (Ratten & Usmanij, 2020). This means that entrepreneurs are alert to opportunities that are evident in the marketplace. Entrepreneurship involves pursuing an idea by focusing on attracting then using resources. Thus, entrepreneurship is a fluid concept that changes over time (Ratten & Jones, 2018). Initially, entrepreneurship is about acquiring the necessary resources to make an idea a reality but once the business has been established it can then be about re-energising or building the business.

Entrepreneurs have a high level of self-efficacy in terms of believing that they can perform a certain task (Ratten & Jones, 2020). This means that, when they come across an innovative idea, they can then respond in a proactive and positive way. Lortie, Cox and Sproul (in press) suggest that there are three main themes regarding how a firm becomes entrepreneurial. Firstly, firms can be entrepreneurial because of their status or due to the personality of the individual running the firm. This means that technology firms are more likely to be classified as entrepreneurial due to the innovative nature of the information, communications and technology industry (Tavares, Santos, Tavares, & Ratten, 2020). A firm might in reality not be entrepreneurial but rather be perceived as being entrepreneurial due to their association with a certain industry. As a result, there are many stereotypes about entrepreneurial firms regarding their business structure. In addition, individuals who are self-starters are perceived as being entrepreneurial due to their quick thinking and ability to start a business.

Secondly, entrepreneurial firms are considered as those that are able to pursue market gaps. This means identifying business opportunities then exploiting them for financial gain. Not all firms are able to act on business opportunities, so an entrepreneurial firm can be differentiated from other firms by their timeliness and capacity for change. Thirdly, entrepreneurial firms perform well in the marketplace. This means that they are able to grow and increase their revenue based on pursuing new growth performance. Performance does not necessarily have to be through financial gain as it can include learning, innovation and social or philanthropic goals. It can be easier to evaluate entrepreneurial firms based on their level of competitive differentiation (Lortie et al., in press). This means that entrepreneurial firms can generally be viewed as firms that focus on their uniqueness in the marketplace. This uniqueness can include differences in branding, service features or network structure. Increasingly entrepreneurial firms are characterised by how new their products or services are compared to previous ones. This means that new products are likely to be substantially different from prior products, thereby valuing innovation as the key product attribute. Entrepreneurial firms are those that disrupt current market practices by bringing new ideas into the market, thereby creating cutting-edge products that include new attributes.

Entrepreneurs are the driving force behind innovation as they provide the impetus for economic development to take place. Entrepreneurs are different from other individuals as they are willing to engage in innovation and risk-taking activity. This occurs by trying new ideas or rethinking current business practices. Some individuals do not want to engage in risk-taking activity and are happy with the status quo. Thus, in order to progress society, entrepreneurs are needed to step in and take decisive action about new projects. It can be difficult for entrepreneurs to introduce new ideas as they are normally untried in the marketplace. This means that there will be some resistance to a new idea until it is adopted by others.

Most types of entrepreneurship emphasise innovation, which is normally measured as "research and development expenditure, number of inventions registered at a patent office, new products and processes introduced. And the share of sales accounted for by innovative products" (Audretsch, 2012: 760). Sometimes growth is used as a proxy for innovation, which is hard to measure. Innovation does not necessarily lead to performance gains and can occur through efficiency improvements. Thus, in order to fully understand the impact of innovation, a holistic perspective is needed that incorporates how entrepreneurship is embedded in communities.

Entrepreneurship in communities

In stagnating or declining regions, local entrepreneurship can spur communities into action. An entrepreneurial mindset involves being alert to opportunities and then taking a risk in pursuing an idea. This can involve leveraging resources in a way to solve problems in the marketplace. Entrepreneurship can provide a way for communities to tackle issues such as deteriorating infrastructure and a shift in population density. When small communities are motivated to be entrepreneurial, the local economy can improve. Therefore, entrepreneurship provides multiple benefits for communities in terms of knowledge spillovers. Whilst business creation is at the centre of most of the entrepreneurial endeavours, other flow-on effects include rising employment rates and regional development. This means that generally entrepreneurs have a sense of commitment to a community in terms of not only providing services but also wanting to facilitate other forms of economic and social activity. In most of the communities, there needs to be a support structure for entrepreneurship. This involves mobilising individuals into action in order to provide economic gain. Communities are important to the entrepreneurial success of a business venture. Entrepreneurship can be considered as a form of economic strategy designed to facilitate community development. A community is dynamic and changes based on the input of individuals, businesses and government entities. Therefore, a community is based on the flow of information circulating in society. The bonds existing amongst individuals in a community can facilitate community development. Economic bonds refer to financial linkages between individuals, businesses or entities based on need. Social bonds refer to more communicative or family networks that provide a sense of cohesion. Individuals in a community have a shared bond due to the locality where they reside.

In order to understand the role of entrepreneurship in communities, it can help to focus on the various elements that comprise a community. This is referred to as the community capitals framework. Adhikari et al. (2018: 259) state that the community capitals framework includes "(1) built, (2) cultural, (3) financial, (4) human, (5) political, (6) social and (7) natural capital". The community capitals framework can be explained as providing a way to analyse community development efforts using a systems perspective. Built capital includes all the physical buildings that are located in an area. These facilities can be used for a variety of purposes including for non-profit and profit reasons. Physical infrastructure is needed for entrepreneurship, so the existence of built capital is required for economic development. Cultural capital includes the history and heritage existing in a region. This type of capital can take time to establish as it involves the use of intangible assets. Financial capital refers to the assets a region has that are in the form of cash or other investment. The more financial capital a region has, the easier it should be for entrepreneurs to obtain financing. Human capital refers to the knowledge and expertise of individuals. This knowledge can be an important source of information for entrepreneurs. Moreover, specific types of expertise such as scientific knowledge may be more conducive to specific types of entrepreneurship. Political capital refers to the accumulation of resources built through relationships. This can include trust and goodwill amongst a group of stakeholders.

Social capital refers to the network of relationships that enables society to function. This includes reciprocity and a sense of belonging in a community. Natural capital involves the existing non-man-made resources such as geographic location, water, energy and mineral resources. Entrepreneurial competencies are embedded within an individual's human capital. This is due to skills such as assessing and exploiting an opportunity being considered as knowledge assets. Over time an individual's entrepreneurial competencies can change through education and training. In addition, the more experience an individual has with certain business pursuits such as acquiring financing or building a venture will contribute to their entrepreneurial competence. Entrepreneurial competencies not only tend to refer to understanding how to recognise then act upon an opportunity but can also refer to self-efficacy or tenacity. This is due to the way an entrepreneur needs to convey a compelling vision about the idea and then manage the risks involved.

The entrepreneurship community is characterised by a lack of knowledge of Indonesia despite its global significance. It is crucial that more emphasis is placed on Indonesian entrepreneurship as it provides a fruitful research stream that is embedded with practical significance. Indonesia is quickly transforming its economy to focus more on technological innovation. Therefore, a greater appreciation of Indonesia's entrepreneurial culture is required. This means that, to understand Indonesian entrepreneurship, the culture and society needs to be appreciated.

Entrepreneurial ecosystems

The literature on entrepreneurial ecosystems has largely developed from the economic geography field. This has resulted in it being more cartographic and structural based than other forms of entrepreneurship. Nevertheless, research on entrepreneurial ecosystems from other research fields particularly in terms of economic advancement has further diversified the research. Entrepreneurial ecosystems involve interdependent relationships that can directly or indirectly support entrepreneurial activity. Cao and Shi (2020: 1) state that "a broadly agreed notion among researchers refers to an entrepreneurial ecosystem as a community of multiple evolving stakeholders that provides a supportive environment for new venture creations within a region". This statement acknowledges that within all entrepreneurial ecosystems is a group of stakeholders that each has a vested interest. Each actor in an entrepreneurial system varies in terms of power and input. More powerful actors include government entities that regulate market behaviour. Less powerful actors include individuals who work for a variety of businesses over a period of time. However, the input that these individuals provide in terms of knowledge and advice can be invaluable.

There has been more interest by Indonesian politicians and business leaders about the relevance of entrepreneurial ecosystems. This is due to the concept of knowledge spillovers being an important component of an entrepreneurial ecosystem. In addition, an ecosystem enables synergies to develop overtime. To create and nurture entrepreneurship, there needs to be an emphasis on innovation and creativity. Entrepreneurship research has shifted from emphasising the individual entrepreneur to taking a more systemic or ecosystem point of view. This derives from the realisation that individuals need a conducive environment to develop their business activities. This environment involves a group of entities working together to achieve a common goal. An entrepreneurial ecosystem functions when a set of coordinated factors work together in order to facilitate productive forms of entrepreneurship. This means that there are positive gains to the entrepreneurial activity in terms of financial and/or social gain. A well-functioning ecosystem has a set of actors that act in a collective manner. Entrepreneurs are not autonomous entities but require others to help meet their goals. This means that networks in the form of exchanges and relationships are important.

An ecosystem is a way to depict the competitive environment. Increasingly firms are depending on other firms in order to create, market and distribute their products. This dependence means that the word ecosystem is replacing the word market in discussions about the business environment. An ecosystem exists as a set of relationships that are based on shared resources, knowledge, spillovers and regulatory requirements. Many different types and sizes of firms are required in an entrepreneurial ecosystem. Startups provide new ideas, whilst large firms can supply access to necessary infrastructure. Thus, the future of Indonesian entrepreneurship faces a clear division between those embracing digital technology and those resisting emerging technologies.

Innovation ecosystems are responsible for much of the disruptive innovation that occurs in society. The nature of these ecosystems differs depending on their location and membership. Normally the location of an ecosystem is related to the type and quantity of specific industry segments. This means that, in places of high-technology or scientific research, there is likely to be associated entities. This makes it easier for entities in an ecosystem to interact and communicate new ideas. The membership of an ecosystem can differ depending on its size. This means that smaller, community-based ecosystems are likely to have local members that can facilitate economic development. Larger ecosystems may have a more varied membership due to the need to incorporate international partners. This makes it difficult in some cases to replicate an ecosystem due to its varied membership. Members of an ecosystem participate in the startup then scale-up of business ventures.

Entrepreneurship is a process that involves bringing into existence ideas that are conceived of with future usages in mind. This means adding an innovation to the marketplace through creative thinking. Individuals choose to become active entrepreneurs. Entrepreneurs face a number of risks when developing their business. The main risk relates to finance in terms of acquiring the right amount and kind of finance. In order to establish and grow a business, financing is needed. Thus, it is important that it is provided in a quick manner. Some entrepreneurs engage in a process of staged investing in order to expend resources only when needed. This means that the business idea is established in a step-by-step way. Other entrepreneurs partner with others in order to share resources and shift the risks.

The role of context in Indonesian entrepreneurship

To fully understand the role Indonesian entrepreneurship plays in the global economy, an examination of the context is needed. Context provides a useful background to analyse entrepreneurship as it influences behaviour and attitudes. Johns (2006: 386) defines context as "the situational opportunities and constraints that affect the occurrence and meaning of organizational behaviour as well as functional relationships between variables". This means that context can occur in both a formal and informal manner. The formal way to analyse context is by examining the impact of economic, social, cultural and technological changes in the environment. This includes analysing formal metrics such as tax rates, regulations and economic growth. Informally context includes the impact of the surrounding environment on entrepreneurship. It may be harder to quantify the impact of informal activity in entrepreneurship. Consequently, incorporating formal and informal contexts into understanding entrepreneurial behaviour is required.

It is important to provide more information about entrepreneurship from an Indonesian context. Context in an entrepreneurial setting refers to "circumstances, conditions, situations or environments that are external to the respective phenomenon and enable or constrain it" (Welter, 2011: 168). Context is important as it can help or hinder entrepreneurship. Some contexts notably geographic areas such as Silicon Valley contain a high proportion of technology firms that help facilitate entrepreneurship. Other locations might constrain entrepreneurship due to regulatory requirements or cultural conditions.

The practice of entrepreneurship in Indonesia varies markedly from that in other countries. Whilst this is gradually changing, there is still some way to go before the conditions are the same that exist in other countries. Due to the impact culture has on entrepreneurial activity, there will always be some differences between countries. In emerging economies, there is normally more necessity rather than opportunity entrepreneurs. This is due to the lack of social security in many emerging economies that makes entrepreneurship a necessity. Moreover, in emerging economies, there can be a lack of institutional structures to facilitate business practices. This can make it difficult for entrepreneurs to gain assurance that they will have legal protection. This means that there is more risk and uncertainty for entrepreneurs.

Entrepreneurship can occur in a variety of contexts that are shaped by biology. This means that environmental conditions in terms of economic conditions shape entrepreneurship, but there are also characteristics of individual entrepreneurs that need to be considered. In addition, there has been an increasing pressure from various stakeholders and institutions in Indonesia to increase rates of entrepreneurship. This has resulted in a changing relationship between business entities, the government and society. More emphasis is now placed on entrepreneurial management and practices that bridge for-profit and non-profit initiatives. Current studies on entrepreneurship in Indonesia focus on a wide range of subjects such as the role of the digital economy, the motivators for adopting an entrepreneurial mindset and the impact of entrepreneurship on society. Yet there seems not to have been an effort to synthesise studies on Indonesian entrepreneurship. In order to guide future research, it is helpful to present the status of this research area as a distinct topic by focusing on the role of context in Indonesian entrepreneurship.

The Indonesian context means that organisations need to be ambidextrous in today's competitive global marketplace. This enables them to align their entrepreneurial practices with emerging market needs. To be ambidextrous can be a complex task as organisations adapt to change in the environment whilst meeting current demands. Organisations need to deal with internal tensions and new issues in order to stay competitive. Ambidexterity can ensure an organisations long-term success by balancing current with future needs. This enables existing management practices to be refined whilst exploring new possibilities. Table 9.1 provides some suggestions for future research in contextual terms. This includes focusing on issues such as inequality, working conditions, international realities and entrepreneurial careers.

Research priorities about Indonesian entrepreneurship

The consideration of entrepreneurship in Indonesia is not a new phenomenon as it has been practised for a long time period. However, this research field will see a new level of interest on the topic given Indonesia's position in the global economy and the increased emphasis within the country on technological innovation. The emerging and potential links between Indonesian entrepreneurship and economic growth tend to be centred around high technology. This incorporates artificial intelligence, mobile commerce and big data that will increase the diversity of Indonesian entrepreneurship research. Due to the increased recognition of Indonesia in the global economy, there is expected to be unprecedented opportunities for researchers. At the same time, there will be challenges to keep

Table 9.1 Suggestions for future research on Indonesian entrepreneurship in contextual terms

Approach	Suggestions for future research
Inequality in entrepreneurship	Study the role of inequality in entrepreneurship. Whether entrepreneurship emerges from need or opportunity. Analyse the role of context in entrepreneurial behaviour.
Working conditions	What are the rewards or incentives for entrepreneurship? Ascertain the different motivations for entrepreneurship. Analyse leadership styles conducive to entrepreneurship.
International realities	Analyse the cultural differences in entrepreneurs. Ascertain how entrepreneurship is embedded in society.
Entrepreneurial careers	Analyse social networks and relationship management. Understand the impact of the formal and informal environment. Evaluate the career expectations of entrepreneurs.

up to date with the rapid changes in the Indonesian economy. This arises from ethical issues in terms of collecting data and issues of intellectual property protection. In addition, there needs to be some degree of consideration about cultural and social factors when doing research in Indonesia. The key opportunity is the promise of a new generation of insights into Indonesian entrepreneurship by means of increased publications. This will enable new research methods, study designs and datasets on Indonesia to be used. In order to progress research on Indonesian entrepreneurship, more conceptual and empirical work is needed. Conceptual work could address the following issues:

1 Types of entrepreneurship occurring in Indonesia
2 Developing a theory of Indonesian entrepreneurship
3 How entrepreneurship can be productive or destructive
4 How technology can support entrepreneurship
5 The role of government and institutional support for entrepreneurship

Each of these distinct research areas will now be discussed in terms of understanding why they are important and how they will contribute to existing entrepreneurship research, thereby offering a new way of understanding how the Indonesian context contributes to economic development. This will enable researchers to focus in more detail on Indonesia as a unique country context for entrepreneurship research and practice.

Types of entrepreneurship occurring in Indonesia

The term 'Indonesian entrepreneurship' might appear ambiguous as it can refer to entrepreneurship in Indonesia and entrepreneurs who are by nationality Indonesian. Entrepreneurship research needs to challenge the current assumptions in order to bring new ideas to fruition. Many of the existing assumptions are ethnocentric and developed by researchers in certain countries. Therefore, entrepreneurship research needs to rethink current research practices by introducing new contexts. This will help encourage serious study of Indonesian entrepreneurship that is needed in order to advance our knowledge about how entrepreneurship is practised.

The relationships between Indonesian culture and entrepreneurship are complex. This is due to the diverse culture existing in Indonesia and the different ways entrepreneurship is conducted in society. Entrepreneurship is motivated by a number of factors including for necessity and those interested in pursuing an opportunity. Thus, research on Indonesian entrepreneurship needs to examine both necessity and opportunity forms of entrepreneurship. Necessity entrepreneurs establish businesses as a source of income in order to survive. Opportunity entrepreneurs are normally not motivated by necessity but instead pursue a gap in the marketplace. Over the past decade, there has been a proliferation of Asian entrepreneurship in general but most of this research focuses on China and India. This means that there is less research specifically on Indonesian entrepreneurship although it is sometimes classified as Southeast Asian entrepreneurship. Thus, more emphasis needs to be placed on examining different types of entrepreneurship.

Developing a theory of Indonesian entrepreneurship

The sheer diversity of existing entrepreneurship studies has contributed to a widening of the field. Entrepreneurship research represents a hybrid field with many different perspectives. Indonesian entrepreneurship is a theme attracting substantial interest in the academic community as it represents a promising research track. Thus, more research needs to develop a theory of Indonesian entrepreneurship as a process of using deliberate action to pursue innovative and risk-taking activity. It involves acknowledging business opportunities that are currently overlooked in the marketplace. Entrepreneurs need to have the confidence and capabilities to turn ideas into a business venture.

The question emerges whether Indonesian entrepreneurship matters. Of course it does, as Indonesia is the fourth most populous country in the world and is at the centre of an emerging entrepreneurial ecosystem. Recent high levels of startup activity especially in the technology sector further fuel this growth. There are many special things about Indonesian entrepreneurship that justify more academic attention. Indonesian entrepreneurs need to not only pursue new ideas but also comply with public interest and business imperatives. Therefore, from their very inception Indonesian startups need to balance different demands. This has meant that the rise in technology startups has also meant a shift in emphasis to digital business. The scope and velocity of change in technology make entrepreneurial outcomes unpredictable for startups. Some startups succeed very quickly, whilst others may need to overcome hurdles in order to develop. This makes it important for startups to depend on creative ideas in order to bring new ideas into the marketplace. The demand for digital products is influenced by the nature of the product and potential revenues. In addition, advertising is supporting digital content development, so digital websites need to appeal to advertisers and consumers.

How entrepreneurship can be productive or destructive

There are environmental factors that pose distinct challenges to Indonesian entrepreneurs, which entrepreneurs in other countries do not face. This exemplifies why the study of Indonesian entrepreneurship is relevant. Developing a definition of Indonesian entrepreneurship is an important step in conceptualising the field in terms of understanding whether entrepreneurship is productive or destructive. Entrepreneurship is defined in different ways that often depend on the interest of the researcher or practitioner. Individuals interest in commercial or corporate ventures tends to define entrepreneurship through financial performance outcomes such as profitability. Those more interested in creativity tend to focus on learning outcomes from entrepreneurial activity. For those invested in social ventures, entrepreneurship tends to be characterised by philanthropic activity. This means that, whilst outcomes are important in entrepreneurial activity, entrepreneurship also involves behaviour or dispositions. Thus, unlike managers who monitor outcomes, entrepreneurs are more fully involved in influencing specific outcomes. Entrepreneurship occurs in a range of contexts but normally involves growth contexts that are identified through the recognition of market opportunity.

How technology can support entrepreneurship

There is more emphasis now in Indonesia on technological forms of entrepreneurship. This is due to the rise of digital startups that have transformed the economy. This means that there are more policy incentives for entrepreneurs to focus on technological innovation. As a result, more research needs to focus on how technological entrepreneurship is occurring in Indonesia. This means focusing on the knowledge economy and the digital revolution.

The role of government and institutional support for entrepreneurship

More research is needed on how government and institutions in Indonesia are influencing entrepreneurship. This includes focusing on the role of entrepreneurial ecosystems in developing smart city initiatives in Indonesia. Local, regional and country level policy needs to be examined in terms of the way entrepreneurship is being encouraged or hindered. This will enable a comparison of policies between geographic regions in order to understand the entrepreneurial environment. Table 9.2 states the future research areas for Indonesian entrepreneurship.

Table 9.2 Future research areas for Indonesian entrepreneurship

Field of study	*Potential research questions*
Anthropology	How does entrepreneurship occur in different contexts in Indonesia?
	What is the emancipatory potential of entrepreneurship for subsistence entrepreneurs in Indonesia?
	What is the role of culture and family-based settings for entrepreneurship?
	What kind of comparative studies will be useful to understand entrepreneurship?
	How have temporal dimensions affected entrepreneurship?
	What are the challenges faced by entrepreneurs due to ethnicity and social class?
	How have institutions and government policy affected entrepreneurship patterns?
	How has the diaspora influenced the growth of business ventures?
	What kind of clusters have affected entrepreneurship?

Future directions

Field of study	Potential research questions
Economics	What kind of financial incentives encourage entrepreneurship? What is the role of tax subsidies in fostering entrepreneurship? How can economic policy be utilised for entrepreneurship reasons? How has internationalisation affected entrepreneurship? What is the role of informal entrepreneurship?
Finance	What kind of financial considerations do Indonesian entrepreneurs make? What are the financial trade-offs in terms of work/life balance for Indonesian entrepreneurs? How do Indonesian entrepreneurs utilise grants and incentives to build their businesses? Are financial or social considerations more important for Indonesian entrepreneurs?
Geography	How does geography influence Indonesian entrepreneurship? Are rural or urban areas more conducive for Indonesian entrepreneurship? What are the socio-economic factors influencing Indonesian entrepreneurs to reside in an area? What is the impact of local government initiatives on Indonesian entrepreneurship?
History	How have Indonesian businesses developed over time? Are Indonesian businesses the same or different from past generations? What is the impact of family on Indonesian entrepreneurs? How have Indonesian businesses changed?
Management	What are the antecedents and consequences of entrepreneurship? How can entrepreneur's stakeholders be managed? What is the role of social class in entrepreneurship? How can longitudinal studies be utilised to understand the changes in entrepreneurship? What is the role of ethnicity in entrepreneurship? How do first, second and third generations of family business owners differ in their response to entrepreneurship?
Organisational behaviour	How are Indonesian businesses structured? What is the typical size of Indonesian business? What kind of business structure is used in Indonesian businesses? How do different generations influence the functioning of Indonesian businesses?
Politics	How does government policy influence Indonesian businesses? What is the impact of taxes, tariffs and other forms of subsidies on Indonesian entrepreneurship? What kind of public/private partnerships exist in Indonesia?
Tourism	What is the impact of tourism on intention to become an entrepreneur? How are tourism ecosystems conducive to entrepreneurship? What kind of tourism enterprises exist in Indonesia?
Technology	What is the impact of technological innovation on Indonesian entrepreneurship? What kind of startups are occurring in Indonesia? How has digital technology influenced Indonesian entrepreneurship?

Research contributions of the book

This chapter seeks to add to the research available on understanding entrepreneurship issues in Indonesia. Previous work on entrepreneurship normally considers regional economic activity or stage of economic development instead of discussing country-level phenomenon. This means that most of the methods used to understand Indonesian entrepreneurship have focused on economic modelling or case study research. These methods provide good data but more integrated methodological approaches would be useful. This would enable research to analyse in fine-grained description how the Indonesian context differs. This would provide a more complex reality of contrasting entrepreneurship contexts, thereby providing insights and directions for future research.

This book consists of a number of chapters on a range of topics related to Indonesian entrepreneurship. Each chapter focuses on a different topic of entrepreneurship such as technology, artisan and education. The field of Indonesian entrepreneurship is new, so care must be taken in ensuring different areas are incorporated into the discussion. This book has developed the field of Indonesian entrepreneurship by synthesising the different areas. There is some degree of personal choice in the topics discussed, but I believe the topics chosen provide the best areas to focus on that combine cultural practices with business ideas.

Due to the continued growth of entrepreneurship in Indonesia, research in this area has not kept pace with practice. Research on entrepreneurship in the Indonesian context has only recently started to emerge in the English language academic journals. Entrepreneurship is viewed as an important strategy to create new business opportunities and to sustain economic development. Therefore, it is timely to examine what entrepreneurship in Indonesia means and what can be done to extend research interest in this topic.

Entrepreneurship can be defined in different ways from the ability to start a business to the knowledge on how to encourage innovative thinking. Thus, it is useful to ask the questions: How should Indonesian entrepreneurship be researched? And what should be the relationships between research and practice? This book has discussed what is known about Indonesian entrepreneurship and what needs to be done. If the underlying area of Indonesian entrepreneurship is optimistic, then, there is a need to understand how Indonesian society can make the most of that potential.

Entrepreneurship in Indonesia is not new but appears to be in a new phase of growth. Nevertheless, the growing research on Indonesian entrepreneurship is yet to coalesce around a common definition. This might be due to the newness of the field and the lack of research coherence. It is also the result of the variety of actions that constitute Indonesian entrepreneurship. This is both a strength in terms of enabling more research on this topic and a weakness in terms of lack of clarity that needs to be addressed. Interest in Indonesian entrepreneurship appears to be cut across mainstream business, civil society and government. This means that this book has explained the multiple dimensions of Indonesian entrepreneurship in a conceptual and empirical way.

Theoretical implications

This book contributes to the research on entrepreneurship in two main ways. First, it reveals a need to focus on emerging country contexts such as Indonesia, thereby highlighting the gap in the entrepreneurship literature in terms of studies on Indonesia. As much of the current entrepreneurship theory is based on a North American or European perspective, it is important to incorporate new country contexts that are based on different cultural conditions. Therefore, this book contributes to the conceptualisation and operationalisation of an Indonesian perspective to entrepreneurship practice. This facilitates the development of new theories that include cultural and historical considerations. This will change entrepreneurship theory by introducing new thought processes into the research discussion. As there are very few entrepreneurship studies on Indonesia in English, this book has opened up the possibility of future research paths. Research on Indonesia is limited in quantity and quality, so this book has taken the first step in reducing this gap. Replication studies can be used in the Indonesian context in order to find out if the current entrepreneurship theory also works in Indonesia. Alternatively new studies that take a fresh approach can be utilised to study entrepreneurship in Indonesia. Second, this book puts forward new ways of understanding Indonesian entrepreneurship. This means that entrepreneurship theory proposed in this book could assist scholars to understand emerging country contexts. China and India have been substantially studied in research on entrepreneurship but few studies focus on Indonesia, thereby including more research on Indonesia can create a better and more holistic understanding of emerging economy entrepreneurship.

Practical contributions of the book

There are a range of topics discussed in this book that highlight the practical importance of Indonesian entrepreneurship. One of the most notable contributions is the discussion about the way entrepreneurs enable change and innovation to occur in a country. This means that it is important for business owners and managers to encourage an entrepreneurial spirit in their business endeavours. This book corroborates earlier studies that advocate for more research on context in entrepreneurship and focus on new country contexts. Entrepreneurship is needed in any context but particularly in emerging markets like Indonesia that are growing quickly and have an increased middle class. Managers need to give more attention to entrepreneurship in Indonesia by cultivating an entrepreneurial culture. Effectively developed policies regarding entrepreneurship can help managers increase their performance.

There are many challenges facing Indonesian managers at the moment including responding to the Covid-19 pandemic. Therefore, utilising an entrepreneurial mindset in business practices can help them deal with uncertainty. Managers are concerned with increasing their business performance but need to do this in a strategic way. Evidence from the literature suggests that managers need to find solutions for a number of problems including low productivity, job stress and dissatisfaction with work practices. Thus, having an entrepreneurial mindset can help managers to balance different needs and to utilise innovative approaches in their business dealings.

Managers should facilitate open communication channels in order to facilitate feedback amongst their stakeholders. This can enable employees, suppliers and customers to communicate their thoughts and concerns. By enabling more participation in decisions, it can help a manager better manage their organisation. This will enable managers to increase their understanding of employees and to address problems. Other management practices such as entrepreneurship training and development can also be implemented. This will enable a more entrepreneurial attitude to be adopted in the workplace. Therefore, a carefully tailored entrepreneurship program based on current needs can facilitate better workplace practices.

Conclusion

This chapter has focused on the future trajectory of research on Indonesian entrepreneurship by enabling new ways of understanding entrepreneurship from a different country context. However, much more work needs to be done on Indonesian entrepreneurship as there is currently a research gap in the academic literature on this topic. Whilst there is much practical evidence of the importance of entrepreneurship in Indonesia, there needs to be more connection between the academic research and practice of entrepreneurship. This book has addressed this gap by highlighting the ample opportunities for research on Indonesian entrepreneurship.

References

Adhikari, R., Bonney, L., Woods, M., Clark, S., Coates, L., Harwood, A., Eversole, R., & Miles, M. (2018). Applying a community entrepreneurship development framework to rural regional development. *Small Enterprise Research*, 25(3), 257–275.

Audretsch, D. B. (2012). Entrepreneurship research. *Management Decision*, 50(5), 755–764.

Cao, Z., & Shi, X. (2020). A systematic literature review of entrepreneurial ecosystems in advanced and emerging economies. *Small Business Economics*, 1–36.

Cavallo, A., Ghezzi, A., & Sanasi, S. (in press). Assessing entrepreneurial ecosystems through a strategic value network approach: Evidence from the San Francisco area. *Journal of Small Business and Enterprise Development*.

Cavusgil, S. T. (2021). Advancing knowledge on emerging markets: Past and future research in perspective. *International Business Review*, 101796.

Johns, G. (2006). The essential impact of context on organizational behavior. *Academy of Management Review*, 31(2), 386–408.

Jones, P., Ratten, V., & Hayduk, T. (2020). Sport, fitness, and lifestyle entrepreneurship. *International Entrepreneurship and Management Journal*, 16(3), 783–793.

Jones, P., Ratten, V., Klapper, R., & Fayolle, A. (2019). Entrepreneurial identity and context: Current trends and an agenda for future research. *The International Journal of Entrepreneurship and Innovation*, *20*(1), 3–7.
Lortie, J., Cox, K., & Sproul, C. (in press). Toward a theory of entrepreneurial differentiation: How entrepreneurial firms compete. *International Entrepreneurship and Management Journal*.
Mendoza-Silva, A. (in press). Innovation capability: A systematic literature review. *European Journal of Innovation Management*.
Ratten, V. (2020a). Coronavirus (Covid-19) and entrepreneurship: Changing life and work landscape. *Journal of Small Business & Entrepreneurship*, *32*(5), 503–516.
Ratten, V. (2020b). Coronavirus and international business: An entrepreneurial ecosystem perspective. *Thunderbird International Business Review*, *62*(5), 629–634.
Ratten, V., & Jones, P. (Eds.). (2018). *Transformational entrepreneurship*. London, UK: Routledge.
Ratten, V., & Jones, P. (2020). New challenges in sport entrepreneurship for value creation. *International Entrepreneurship and Management Journal*, *16*(3), 961–980.
Ratten, V., & Usmanij, P. (2020). Entrepreneurship education: Time for a change in research direction? *The International Journal of Management Education*, 100367.
Tavares, F., Santos, E., Tavares, V., & Ratten, V. (2020). The perception and knowledge of financial risk of the Portuguese. *Sustainability*, *12*(19), 8255.
Welter, F. (2011). Contextualizing entrepreneurship – Conceptual challenges and ways forward. *Entrepreneurship Theory and Practice*, *35*(1), 165–184.
Zhao, W., Ritchie, J. B., & Echtner, C. M. (2011). Social capital and tourism entrepreneurship. *Annals of Tourism Research*, *38*(4), 1570–1593.

Index

active learning 5
agricultural 3, 103–106, 109, 111
ambiguity 4, 9, 24, 81
archipelago 3, 61, 92, 115
Asia 1, 2, 32, 57, 60, 75, 79, 115, 116
Asian 1, 2, 115, 124, 125

Bali 3, 34, 67, 70, 92
Bangladesh 60, 62
bankruptcy 5
Buddhists 3
business practices 21, 51, 54, 78, 106, 118, 122, 129
business relationships 3, 115

Catholicism 93, 115
China 1, 6, 16, 60, 61, 100
colonial government 62
community 7, 9, 10, 15, 19, 21, 24, 25, 26, 34, 35, 38, 40–42, 48, 53, 54, 58–60, 63, 64, 66, 68, 70, 72, 86, 105, 110, 114, 119–121, 125
competitive 12, 23, 24, 35, 37, 39, 45, 49, 79, 81–83, 88, 93, 105, 106, 118, 121, 123
construction sector 62
Covid-19 11, 12, 20, 26, 29, 79, 104, 129
cultural conditions 2, 20, 109, 116, 122, 129

data analytics 11, 78, 88
databases 94, 100
democracy 3
demographic conditions 94
demography 95
Denmark 94
diaspora 58, 59, 61, 72, 116, 126

economic activity 1, 15, 26, 36, 92, 128
emerging markets 4, 6, 7, 23, 116, 129
environmental challenges 8
ethnic groups 2, 34, 61, 115
ethnic migrant entrepreneurs 57, 59, 60, 74
Europe 1, 9, 99
expatriates 57, 67

failure 5, 11, 83, 95, 96, 98, 99
farmers 27, 42, 105, 106, 111
fertile soil 3
financial capital 119
Finland 94
foreign direct investment 6
forest 3

gender 4, 25, 63, 64, 96, 98, 99
Germany 59, 94
global entrepreneurship 94
global mobility 57
God 3, 35
government 3, 10, 24, 26, 51, 62, 66, 83, 93, 94, 109, 111, 114, 119, 120, 122, 124, 126–128
grief 5
gross domestic product 3, 92

Hindu 3, 35, 48, 61, 93, 115
historical setting 7
hospitality 3, 26
host countries 58, 59
human connections 7
human interaction 7, 105
humanity 3, 109

income generating 8
independence 2, 4, 20, 37, 115

India 1, 6, 60, 61, 115, 124, 129
inflation 92
innovation mapping 11
insolvency 5
international strategies 5, 6
internet 7, 11, 21, 38, 78, 85, 88, 89, 110
intra-regional 69, 75, 95
Iran 95
Israel 94
Italian 59

Jakarta 2, 92, 115
Javanese 2, 28, 48, 62

Komodo 3

leadership style 89, 95, 123
locations 4, 38, 40, 70, 104, 122
Lombok 3
low-skilled workers 57

Malay 2, 61
Malaysian 61
marketing 20, 23, 24, 26, 32, 38, 49, 74, 78, 87–89, 93, 100, 116
marriage 61, 69, 72
mature economy 6
middle class 2, 3, 7, 116, 129
migrant-receiving 57, 58, 60, 63–67, 72, 74
mining 3
monsoon 3
Muslim 3, 34
Myanmar 60, 61

nascent entrepreneurship 94
Nepal 61
new ventures 1
North America 1

Papua New Guinea 2
passion 9, 21, 32, 35–37, 41
performance gains 105, 118
phenomenon 7, 11
Philippines 60–62, 79

plantation 3
political reform 1, 6, 8, 54, 58, 59, 62, 65, 66, 73, 86, 94, 116, 119
poverty 2, 23, 194, 108, 114
proactiveness 3, 37
psychological 4, 5, 39, 40
public information 57

quality controls 95

real world 11, 78
regional development 1, 8, 15, 119
regulatory contexts 59
resilience 11
roads 7
Romania 95
rurality 103

school 9, 10, 94
sensemaking 5, 24
social regulations 94
social responsibility 105, 111
societal diversity 57
societal problems 11, 107, 110
socio-cultural context 58
socio-economic factors 4, 127
Sundanese 2
survey 66, 94, 95

technical skills 93
tertiary education 94
Thailand 59–61, 79, 96
theoretical framework 58
theories 1, 6, 114, 116, 129
trade association 63, 64, 67
trust 3, 6, 47, 51, 69, 70, 72, 87, 100, 119

uncertainty 11, 51, 89, 117, 122, 129
United Kingdom 94
United States 94

volcanic activity 2

weather 6, 42, 104
World Bank 58, 60, 61